# SMB: File Sharing and Network Security

James Relington

# DEDICATION

To those who seek knowledge, inspiration, and new perspectives—
may this book be a companion on your journey, a spark for curiosity,
and a reminder that every page turned is a step toward discovery.

# AKNOWLEDGEMENTS

I would like to express my deepest gratitude to everyone who contributed to the creation of this book. To my colleagues and mentors, your insights and expertise have been invaluable. A special thank you to my family and friends for their unwavering support and encouragement throughout this journey.

# Introduction to SMB: Concepts and Evolution

The Server Message Block (SMB) protocol is one of the most widely used methods for network file sharing, allowing applications and users to read, create, update, and delete files on remote servers. It also enables devices to communicate for various functions such as printing and interprocess communication within a network. Originally developed in the 1980s by IBM, SMB has undergone a significant evolution, adapting to the rapidly changing landscape of enterprise IT and network security.

At its core, SMB was designed to provide a way for systems to share access to files, printers, and serial ports within a local area network (LAN). The early days of network computing called for a protocol that could offer seamless file sharing between different systems in an office environment. IBM's original implementation aimed to make these resources available over a network in much the same way as they would be on a local disk. Microsoft quickly recognized the potential of SMB and adapted it for its own operating systems, where it became an essential component of the Windows networking stack.

As networking grew beyond LANs to include wide-area networks (WANs) and eventually the internet, SMB faced new challenges that required enhancements and revisions. Microsoft took the lead in SMB development and introduced several updates that transformed the protocol into a more secure and efficient system. With the release of Windows NT, SMB became deeply integrated with Windows' core networking functionality. The collaboration between Microsoft and Intel led to the Common Internet File System (CIFS) standard, which is sometimes used interchangeably with SMB, though CIFS refers specifically to a particular dialect of SMB.

Throughout the 1990s and early 2000s, SMB was widely adopted due to its integration with Windows environments, which dominated business and enterprise networks during that era. However, as networks grew larger and more interconnected, security became a significant concern. The original SMB versions lacked many of the safeguards that are considered mandatory today, such as encryption and message signing. This left SMB traffic vulnerable to interception, tampering, and attacks such as man-in-the-middle (MITM) exploits.

Recognizing the limitations of early versions, Microsoft introduced SMB 2.0 with Windows Vista and Windows Server 2008. This marked a pivotal moment in the protocol's history. SMB 2.0 brought substantial improvements, including reduced command complexity, greater efficiency by allowing multiple requests within the same connection, and enhanced scalability to accommodate larger enterprise environments. It also began addressing the need for stronger security mechanisms, although it was not until later versions that these measures became more comprehensive.

The release of SMB 3.0 alongside Windows 8 and Windows Server 2012 represented another significant leap forward. SMB 3.0 introduced vital security features such as end-to-end encryption, which protected data in transit from eavesdropping and unauthorized access. SMB Direct, another feature of SMB 3.0, enabled faster data transfers using Remote Direct Memory Access (RDMA), dramatically improving performance for high-throughput applications like virtualization and database services.

Further enhancements continued with SMB 3.02 and SMB 3.1.1. SMB 3.1.1, introduced with Windows 10 and Windows Server 2016, included pre-authentication integrity checks that helped mitigate interception and spoofing attacks, thereby reinforcing trust between client and server during the initial handshake process. Additionally, SMB 3.1.1 supported more advanced encryption algorithms, reflecting the growing need for resilient data protection in enterprise and cloud environments.

While Microsoft has been the primary force behind SMB's development, the protocol has extended far beyond Windows networks. Open-source implementations like Samba have allowed Linux and Unix systems to communicate with Windows systems using the SMB protocol. This cross-platform capability has made SMB an indispensable tool for mixed-OS environments, supporting countless organizations where interoperability is critical.

SMB's longevity can be attributed to its flexibility and continual adaptation to new technological demands. As cloud services and hybrid IT architectures become more prevalent, SMB continues to evolve to meet modern expectations. Its integration with platforms like Microsoft Azure and Amazon FSx demonstrates its ability to bridge on-premises and cloud-based storage infrastructures.

Despite its advancements, SMB remains a popular target for cyber threats, primarily because of its ubiquity and the existence of legacy systems still running outdated versions of the protocol. High-profile incidents, such as the WannaCry ransomware attack in 2017, exploited vulnerabilities in SMBv1, prompting a worldwide push to disable or replace the older version with more secure alternatives.

Today, SMB's development is closely aligned with broader trends in cybersecurity and enterprise networking. Features such as SMB over QUIC, which tunnels SMB traffic through encrypted HTTPS/3 connections, aim to further secure SMB traffic, especially for remote work scenarios where traditional VPNs may introduce latency or complexity.

SMB is no longer just a file-sharing protocol; it has become an essential component of enterprise network infrastructure, balancing performance, security, and compatibility. Its historical journey from a simple file-sharing mechanism to a sophisticated, secure, and scalable protocol reflects the broader evolution of IT systems and network security over the past four decades. As organizations continue to modernize their networks and adapt to emerging technologies, SMB's ability to evolve will ensure its relevance for years to come.

# The Role of SMB in Modern Networks

In the landscape of modern networks, the Server Message Block (SMB) protocol plays a critical role as a backbone for file sharing, resource access, and inter-device communication. Its presence is deeply embedded in the daily operations of businesses, enterprises, and even home networks. As organizations become more interconnected and dependent on seamless data exchange, SMB has maintained its position as a trusted method for facilitating collaboration, managing storage, and enabling critical business functions across different platforms and systems.

At its essence, SMB allows devices within a network to share files and resources, such as printers and serial ports, with ease. This seemingly simple capability forms the foundation for many business operations. Employees in offices around the world rely on shared folders hosted on central servers to collaborate on projects, exchange information, and store important documentation. In environments where fast and reliable access to shared data is essential, SMB ensures that files can be accessed as if they were stored locally, even when they reside on remote servers. This capability helps streamline workflows and reduces the need for redundant copies of data to be scattered across individual machines.

The role of SMB in modern networks extends beyond basic file sharing. It is integral to the functioning of critical services such as Distributed File System (DFS), which allows multiple SMB shares to be grouped into a single logical namespace. This abstraction simplifies data access for end-users, enabling them to navigate complex storage environments without needing to know the specific physical locations of files. For IT administrators, SMB combined with DFS facilitates centralized management and better utilization of available storage resources, contributing to more efficient and organized network infrastructures.

Moreover, SMB is an enabler of centralized authentication and access control. When integrated with directory services like Microsoft Active Directory, SMB provides a robust framework for managing user permissions and enforcing security policies. By tying file share access to domain credentials, organizations can ensure that only authorized users can interact with specific data or network resources. This centralized control mechanism not only enhances security but also simplifies user management, especially in large environments with hundreds or thousands of employees.

Modern networks are no longer confined to physical offices or static LANs. The shift towards remote work, cloud computing, and hybrid architectures has required SMB to adapt to new operational models. In this context, SMB serves as a bridge between on-premises systems and cloud services. Platforms like Microsoft Azure Files and Amazon FSx for Windows File Server leverage SMB to deliver cloud-based file shares that are compatible with traditional Windows-based applications. This seamless integration between cloud storage and on-premises networks allows organizations to extend their existing IT investments while embracing modern, scalable cloud infrastructure.

SMB's versatility is further demonstrated by its role in supporting virtualization and data center operations. Virtual machines (VMs) often rely on SMB for accessing shared storage, particularly in Hyper-V environments where SMB 3.0 and later versions enable efficient data access via SMB Direct and SMB Multichannel. By reducing latency and supporting high-throughput workloads, SMB ensures that virtualized environments perform optimally, contributing to the overall stability and responsiveness of modern data centers.

The protocol also plays a pivotal role in enabling secure communication within networks. Security enhancements introduced in newer versions of SMB, such as end-to-end encryption and integrity signing, provide robust protection for sensitive data as it traverses the network. These features are critical in modern IT environments where cyber threats are increasingly sophisticated, and data privacy is a top priority. By encrypting SMB traffic, organizations can safeguard their information from unauthorized access, even if attackers manage to intercept network packets.

Another aspect of SMB's role in contemporary networks is its impact on user experience. End-users expect fast and reliable access to shared files, regardless of their physical location or the device they are using. Modern implementations of SMB, such as SMB 3.1.1, are optimized for performance, providing features like large maximum transmission units (MTUs), persistent handles, and advanced caching mechanisms. These enhancements reduce latency and improve reliability, ensuring that users can access and edit files without encountering delays or disconnections. This is especially important in distributed work environments where employees collaborate across different time zones and geographic regions.

The protocol's flexibility in supporting cross-platform compatibility is another crucial element of its role in modern networks. Thanks to open-source projects like Samba, SMB can be implemented on non-Windows systems, allowing Linux and Unix servers to participate fully in Windows-based file sharing ecosystems. This capability is essential for organizations that operate heterogeneous IT environments, where seamless communication and interoperability between different operating systems are non-negotiable.

Additionally, SMB serves as a key enabler of automation and orchestration in modern IT workflows. System administrators can automate routine tasks such as provisioning new shares, setting permissions, and monitoring usage metrics using PowerShell scripts or other management tools that interface with SMB shares. This automation reduces manual effort, minimizes human error, and ensures consistent application of policies across the network.

As businesses continue to demand greater agility, scalability, and resilience from their IT infrastructures, SMB's ability to integrate with emerging technologies is critical. New developments, such as SMB over QUIC, position the protocol to function efficiently over unreliable or high-latency networks by encapsulating SMB traffic within secure and resilient HTTPS/3 tunnels. This is particularly valuable for remote workers and branch offices, where traditional VPN solutions may fall short in terms of speed or user experience.

SMB's enduring presence in modern networks is a testament to its adaptability and robustness. It remains a fundamental building block for file and resource sharing across countless organizations worldwide, providing the foundation for collaboration, secure communication, and streamlined operations. As networks become increasingly complex and distributed, SMB continues to evolve, meeting the demands of both legacy systems and cutting-edge technologies. Its role has expanded far beyond its original scope, making it an indispensable protocol in the ongoing development of modern IT ecosystems.

# SMB Protocol Versions and Compatibility

The SMB protocol has undergone several major revisions since its inception, each version bringing new capabilities, performance enhancements, and security features that reflect the evolving needs of network environments. Understanding the progression of SMB versions is essential to comprehending its compatibility challenges and the overall dynamics of file sharing in modern networks. As networks have expanded beyond traditional local area networks to include complex enterprise, hybrid, and cloud infrastructures, SMB has adapted to meet these demands while maintaining a degree of backward compatibility with older systems.

The earliest widely used iteration of SMB was SMB 1.0, often referred to as the CIFS (Common Internet File System) dialect. Introduced by Microsoft in the early 1990s, SMB 1.0 quickly became the standard for file and printer sharing in Windows-based environments. While functional and simple, SMB 1.0 was designed for small networks with limited security requirements. It offered basic file-sharing capabilities but lacked modern performance optimization and security measures. SMB 1.0 relied on the NetBIOS protocol for name resolution and transport over TCP/IP networks, which introduced additional overhead and complexity in larger networks. Over time, the limitations of SMB 1.0 became apparent, particularly as enterprises demanded higher throughput and stronger security.

The introduction of SMB 2.0 with Windows Vista and Windows Server 2008 marked a substantial shift in the protocol's evolution. SMB 2.0 was a complete redesign aimed at addressing the inefficiencies and security gaps of its predecessor. It dramatically reduced the number of commands used by the protocol, streamlining communication between clients and servers. Features such as pipelining, where multiple requests could be sent without waiting for a response, and larger buffer sizes, significantly improved performance, especially in high-latency environments. SMB 2.0 also introduced support for symbolic links and durable file handles, which were particularly valuable for server failover and reconnection scenarios.

Following SMB 2.0, Microsoft introduced SMB 2.1 with Windows 7 and Windows Server 2008 R2. This incremental upgrade included enhancements such as improved scalability for concurrent open files and the introduction of leasing mechanisms that allowed clients to cache file data more effectively, reducing network traffic and improving application responsiveness. While SMB 2.1 retained compatibility with SMB 2.0, the improvements made it better suited for enterprise deployments with high user counts and demanding workloads.

SMB 3.0 arrived alongside Windows 8 and Windows Server 2012, marking a significant advancement in the protocol's security and performance capabilities. One of the most notable innovations in SMB 3.0 was the introduction of SMB encryption, enabling the protection of data in transit without requiring a VPN or IPsec. This feature was a direct response to the growing need for secure communication over potentially untrusted networks. Additionally, SMB 3.0 brought SMB Multichannel, allowing multiple network connections to be used simultaneously for a single session, thereby increasing throughput and ensuring fault tolerance. SMB Direct, leveraging RDMA-capable network adapters, further enhanced performance by enabling low-latency, high-speed data transfers with minimal CPU overhead.

SMB 3.02, introduced with Windows 8.1 and Windows Server 2012 R2, delivered refinements to existing features. These included improved support for continuous availability of applications in clustered environments and enhanced scalability for larger enterprise deployments. SMB 3.02 optimized the resilience of file shares and introduced minor adjustments to SMB Multichannel and SMB Direct to provide greater stability and performance.

The next major milestone was SMB 3.1.1, released with Windows 10 and Windows Server 2016. This version introduced pre-authentication integrity, a crucial security measure that helped prevent man-in-the-middle attacks by verifying the integrity of the SMB session setup before authentication. SMB 3.1.1 also mandated the use of stronger encryption algorithms, including AES-128-GCM, to provide even better protection against modern cryptographic attacks. While maintaining backward compatibility with previous SMB 3.x versions, SMB 3.1.1 focused heavily on improving security for organizations adopting zero-trust models and hybrid cloud infrastructures.

Each new version of SMB has been designed with backward compatibility in mind, ensuring that newer clients can still communicate with servers running older versions of the protocol. However, this compatibility is not without its challenges. For instance, SMB 3.0 clients can negotiate down to SMB 2.1 or SMB 2.0 when connecting to servers that do not support the newer dialects. While this flexibility helps maintain functionality in mixed-version environments, it can also inadvertently expose networks to vulnerabilities inherent in older protocol versions, such as SMB 1.0's lack of encryption and susceptibility to attacks like EternalBlue.

In recent years, Microsoft and other industry leaders have recommended disabling SMB 1.0 wherever possible due to its critical security flaws and lack of modern protections. Many organizations have transitioned to using only SMB 2.x or SMB 3.x for their internal file sharing and application needs. However, the need for compatibility with legacy systems still presents challenges. Many industrial control systems, embedded devices, and older applications may only support SMB 1.0, forcing businesses to maintain isolated environments or find alternative solutions until those systems can be upgraded or replaced.

The introduction of SMB over QUIC represents the latest stage in the protocol's evolution, designed to address modern networking demands such as secure remote access without the need for traditional VPNs. By encapsulating SMB traffic within QUIC and HTTPS/3, SMB over QUIC offers a more resilient and encrypted transport layer for accessing file shares in distributed and mobile workforces. Although SMB over QUIC is not yet as universally adopted as traditional SMB 3.1.1, it signifies the protocol's trajectory towards cloud-native and remote-first architectures.

Compatibility considerations extend beyond Microsoft's ecosystem. With the open-source Samba project, SMB can also be deployed on Linux and Unix systems, allowing them to interact with Windows environments. Samba has kept pace with SMB developments, supporting many of the key features introduced in SMB 2.x and SMB 3.x, including encryption and Active Directory integration. This cross-platform capability is essential in today's diverse IT landscapes, where seamless interoperability between Windows and non-Windows systems is often critical to business operations.

As SMB continues to evolve, understanding the nuances of its different versions and compatibility implications is crucial for network administrators and security professionals. Selecting the appropriate SMB version for specific use cases, enforcing security best practices, and maintaining awareness of potential downgrade vulnerabilities are all essential components of a robust network strategy that balances functionality, performance, and security in modern infrastructures.

# How SMB Facilitates File Sharing

The Server Message Block (SMB) protocol is fundamentally designed to enable efficient and seamless file sharing across networked environments, serving as a bridge between users and the resources they need. Its ability to facilitate file sharing lies in the protocol's ability to standardize how clients and servers communicate with one another to access, read, write, and manage files located on remote systems. SMB turns what could be a complex task of coordinating file access between multiple systems into a transparent and user-friendly process that mirrors local file interactions.

At the heart of SMB's file-sharing capability is its client-server architecture. In a typical SMB implementation, a client sends a request to an SMB server to access shared resources, which could include files, directories, or printers. The server evaluates the request, applies relevant permissions and access control policies, and responds accordingly. The interaction is designed to be seamless from the user's perspective. For instance, when a user maps a network drive or accesses a shared folder via their file explorer, they are in fact engaging with the SMB protocol behind the scenes to communicate with the remote server.

SMB simplifies file sharing by allowing remote files to be treated as if they were stored locally. This means that users can perform standard operations like opening, editing, saving, deleting, or moving files directly from a remote location without needing to download and re-upload them manually. By handling these operations through a well-defined set of commands and responses, SMB reduces latency and enhances productivity, particularly in collaborative environments where multiple users need to access and work on shared documents simultaneously.

The protocol supports a range of commands tailored to different aspects of file sharing and resource management. These include file open and close requests, read and write commands, directory queries, and file locking mechanisms. One of the key strengths of SMB is its implementation of file and byte-range locking, which prevents data corruption and ensures consistency when multiple users attempt to access the same file concurrently. By locking an entire file or specific ranges of data within a file, SMB helps manage access conflicts and protects the integrity of shared information.

SMB also supports the sharing of entire directories or network shares, which are typically mapped to a designated folder or storage volume on the server. These shares are exposed to clients via a network path, often in the form of UNC (Universal Naming Convention) paths such as \ServerName\ShareName. This abstraction allows users to access files across the network without needing to know the specific physical location of the data on the server's file system. The simplicity of UNC paths makes it easy for users to connect to and interact with shared resources, while system administrators retain control over how those resources are configured and accessed.

A critical component of SMB file sharing is its integration with authentication and authorization mechanisms. When a client attempts to access an SMB share, the protocol enforces security by requiring user credentials to be validated against the server's authentication system, typically integrated with directory services like Active Directory. Once authenticated, the user's access to shared files and folders is governed by access control lists (ACLs) and share-level permissions, which define what actions the user is allowed to perform. These security controls are granular, enabling administrators to enforce read-only or full-control access rights on a per-user or per-group basis.

SMB is designed to handle both small-scale and enterprise-level deployments, where file sharing extends across multiple geographic locations and large user bases. In such environments, SMB can be paired with technologies like Distributed File System (DFS) to create a unified namespace that aggregates multiple file shares under a single logical hierarchy. This eliminates the need for users to remember multiple share locations or server addresses, simplifying the overall user experience and improving operational efficiency.

To further enhance file-sharing performance, SMB incorporates a variety of optimizations. Features such as pipelining and request batching allow multiple operations to be sent to the server before receiving responses, reducing the overhead associated with traditional request-response models. SMB Multichannel, introduced in SMB 3.0, takes this a step further by enabling the use of multiple network interfaces simultaneously, thereby improving throughput and providing redundancy. These enhancements are particularly valuable in data-intensive scenarios such as media production, database access, and large-scale collaborative projects.

SMB also leverages advanced caching mechanisms to minimize unnecessary network traffic and improve responsiveness. For example, SMB leasing allows clients to cache file metadata and read-only data locally, reducing the frequency of repeated queries to the server. This results in faster file access times for users and decreased load on the server, especially in environments where files are frequently read but seldom modified.

Beyond file-level operations, SMB facilitates directory services by enabling clients to browse shared folders and enumerate directory contents. This capability is crucial for users to navigate through remote file structures and locate the resources they need. SMB's support for metadata queries allows users to retrieve information such as file size, creation dates, and permissions without opening the file itself, further streamlining workflows.

Security remains a focal point in how SMB facilitates file sharing. Modern versions of the protocol, such as SMB 3.0 and later, support encryption to protect data as it traverses the network. This ensures that even if SMB traffic is intercepted, the data remains unreadable to unauthorized parties. Additionally, integrity checks built into the protocol help verify that data has not been tampered with during transmission, reinforcing trust between clients and servers.

The role of SMB in enabling file sharing extends to hybrid and cloud environments. Solutions like Azure Files and Amazon FSx integrate SMB shares into cloud storage services, allowing organizations to maintain familiar SMB workflows while benefiting from the scalability and flexibility of cloud infrastructure. This allows enterprises to extend on-premises file sharing capabilities to remote offices and mobile workforces without sacrificing compatibility or performance.

Ultimately, SMB remains a cornerstone of network file sharing, balancing ease of use, performance, and security. Its ability to facilitate seamless interaction with remote files, enforce fine-grained access controls, and integrate with modern IT infrastructure makes it an indispensable tool for organizations across industries. Whether within a single office LAN or across global networks, SMB continues to deliver the reliable and efficient file-sharing functionality that modern users and businesses depend on every day.

## SMB vs. Other File Sharing Protocols

The Server Message Block (SMB) protocol has long been a cornerstone of file sharing, especially within Windows-based networks, but it exists in an ecosystem populated by several other file-sharing protocols that serve different purposes, platforms, and environments. Understanding how SMB compares to these alternatives offers insight into why certain organizations and industries may choose one protocol over another, depending on their specific needs regarding performance, security, cross-platform compatibility, and ease of integration. The differences between SMB and protocols such as Network File System (NFS), File Transfer Protocol (FTP), Secure File Transfer Protocol (SFTP), and Web Distributed Authoring and Versioning (WebDAV) highlight the various strengths and limitations of each technology.

SMB stands out primarily for its tight integration with Microsoft Windows environments. Designed originally to facilitate file and printer sharing between computers on local area networks, SMB has evolved into a fully-featured protocol that supports secure file transfers, resource access, and even remote procedure calls. One of SMB's most significant advantages is its deep integration with Windows operating systems and Active Directory services, allowing for streamlined authentication, group policy enforcement, and user rights management. This close relationship with Windows systems makes SMB the de facto standard for most organizations operating within a Microsoft-centric IT ecosystem.

In contrast, NFS, which was originally developed by Sun Microsystems, is more prevalent in Unix and Linux environments. While both SMB and NFS provide network-based access to remote files as if they were stored locally, NFS tends to offer more seamless integration within Linux-based systems due to its native support in most Unix-like operating systems. NFS operates using a stateless protocol model, which means the server does not retain session information about clients. This can offer performance benefits and greater resilience in certain network conditions. However, traditional NFS versions lack some of the advanced security features inherent in modern SMB implementations, such as encryption and session signing, unless supplemented with additional security layers like Kerberos.

SMB also differs from FTP, which has historically been one of the most common methods for transferring files over TCP/IP networks. FTP is a simple, straightforward protocol that allows users to upload and download files from a remote server. However, FTP does not inherently provide file locking, remote editing capabilities, or integration with native file explorers in operating systems. SMB allows users to open, modify, and save remote files directly as if they were working on local drives, whereas FTP generally requires files to be downloaded, edited locally, and then re-uploaded to the server. Additionally, FTP's security is relatively weak by modern standards, as it typically transmits data and credentials in plain text unless paired with secure variants such as FTPS or replaced by protocols like SFTP.

SFTP, which operates over SSH, offers improved security compared to traditional FTP by providing encrypted data transfers and secure authentication mechanisms. While SFTP is commonly used in scenarios where security is paramount, such as transferring sensitive files between business partners or accessing remote servers over untrusted networks, it lacks the broader functionality of SMB in terms of shared resource access and direct file manipulation through network drives. SFTP is primarily designed for transferring files, not for providing an interactive file system where files can be opened and edited in place by multiple users, which is a core strength of SMB in collaborative environments.

Another protocol often compared to SMB is WebDAV, an extension of HTTP that enables users to collaboratively edit and manage files stored on remote web servers. WebDAV allows files to be mapped as network drives and accessed through native file explorers, much like SMB. However, WebDAV's foundation in HTTP gives it certain advantages when navigating firewalls and proxies, as HTTP traffic is generally permitted on most corporate networks. Nevertheless, WebDAV is limited in its ability to handle large-scale enterprise file sharing, and it lacks the advanced security features and performance optimizations found in modern SMB versions, such as SMB Multichannel or SMB Direct.

Performance is another area where differences between SMB and other protocols become apparent. SMB 3.0 and later versions incorporate features designed to enhance data transfer speed and resilience. For example, SMB Multichannel allows multiple network connections to be used simultaneously, increasing throughput and providing failover capabilities in case of network interface card (NIC) failures. SMB Direct leverages Remote Direct Memory Access (RDMA) to significantly reduce latency and CPU usage during large file transfers, making SMB highly suitable for data-intensive operations such as virtualization, big data workloads, and enterprise database management. While NFS and SFTP are reliable for general file transfers, they typically lack these high-performance capabilities out of the box.

Another important consideration is how well these protocols integrate with security and identity management systems. SMB's integration with Active Directory makes it easier to enforce granular access controls using Group Policy Objects and Access Control Lists. This is a key advantage for organizations that require tight control over who can access or modify shared files. While NFS can be integrated with directory services like LDAP and Kerberos, this often requires additional configuration and management effort, particularly in mixed-OS environments where both Windows and Linux systems coexist. SFTP, relying on SSH authentication, can be highly secure but is generally more suited to one-time file transfers or automated batch jobs rather than persistent, collaborative file access.

SMB also provides superior user experience within Windows environments. Mapping network drives through SMB is a simple, intuitive process, and the protocol supports native file and printer sharing capabilities, seamless drive redirection, and easy browsing of shared folders via Windows Explorer. In contrast, while WebDAV and FTP allow for some level of drive mapping or browsing, they often require additional client software or browser plugins to function optimally, and they may not offer the same level of responsiveness or file system integration as SMB does in Windows-based networks.

In mixed-platform environments, where both Windows and Unix-like systems coexist, organizations often have to weigh the benefits of SMB against NFS or implement both protocols depending on the workflow. For example, SMB may be used for Windows workstations that need access to corporate file shares, while NFS may be used by backend Linux servers or developers working in Unix-based environments. Samba, the open-source implementation of SMB, has been instrumental in bridging this gap by allowing Linux and Unix servers to act as SMB servers or clients, thereby providing cross-platform file sharing capabilities without sacrificing compatibility.

Ultimately, the choice between SMB and other file-sharing protocols depends on a variety of factors, including operating system preferences, performance requirements, security considerations, and administrative overhead. SMB offers a comprehensive solution that balances ease of use, advanced features, and strong security, particularly in Microsoft-centric networks, while protocols like NFS,

SFTP, FTP, and WebDAV each present their own unique strengths in specific use cases. The diversity of available file-sharing protocols ensures that organizations can tailor their infrastructure to meet the unique needs of their users and operational environments, often combining multiple protocols to achieve the desired balance of functionality and flexibility.

# Network Topologies Supporting SMB

The Server Message Block (SMB) protocol is designed to function effectively across a wide range of network topologies, each of which presents unique characteristics that influence how SMB operates. The underlying network topology can have a significant impact on the performance, reliability, and security of SMB communications. As organizations have grown and network environments have evolved, SMB has been adapted to work in everything from small office LANs to large-scale enterprise networks, hybrid clouds, and distributed wide-area networks (WANs).

One of the most common network topologies supporting SMB is the traditional star topology, where all devices are connected to a central switch or hub. In this setup, SMB servers and clients communicate through this central network device, which acts as the traffic coordinator. The star topology is widely favored in small to medium-sized businesses and many corporate environments due to its simplicity, ease of management, and fault isolation. If a single client node fails or becomes disconnected, it does not impact the other nodes or the SMB server. Within a star topology, SMB's file sharing and resource access capabilities benefit from the relatively low latency and high bandwidth provided by modern switches and routers.

Another network design that supports SMB well is the extended star topology, where multiple star networks are interconnected via additional switches or routers, forming a larger structure. This type of topology is often deployed in larger organizations with several departments or buildings that require independent local networks while still being interconnected. SMB functions effectively in extended star environments by leveraging TCP/IP to transmit data between clients and servers residing in different segments of the network. Modern SMB versions, such as SMB 3.x, enhance this with features like SMB Multichannel, which allows multiple network interfaces on clients and servers to be used concurrently, maximizing throughput and providing redundancy in case of network failures.

SMB also operates within bus and ring topologies, although these are less common in modern network designs. In a bus topology, all nodes share a single communication line or backbone. While simple and cost-effective, bus networks suffer from performance limitations and signal collisions as more devices are added. SMB traffic on bus topologies can experience delays due to the shared nature of the network medium, leading to bottlenecks during periods of high usage. Similarly, ring topologies, where devices are connected in a circular fashion, allow SMB communication to travel in one or both directions around the ring. While ring networks can offer fault tolerance if configured with dual rings, they are less common in today's Ethernet-dominated environments, where star and mesh designs prevail.

In larger enterprise environments, mesh and partial mesh topologies are increasingly common, especially in data centers and distributed network infrastructures. In a full mesh topology, each node is connected directly to every other node, ensuring multiple paths for SMB traffic to traverse between clients and servers. This redundancy enhances fault tolerance and load balancing, which is particularly beneficial in high-availability environments where SMB servers must deliver uninterrupted access to critical files and applications. A partial mesh topology, where only selected nodes have multiple connections, can strike a balance between cost and resilience while still supporting the scalability needed for SMB traffic in large organizations.

Campus networks, which span multiple buildings or even entire campuses, often use hierarchical or layered topologies to facilitate SMB communication. These networks typically consist of core, distribution, and access layers, each responsible for specific roles in traffic management. At the core layer, high-speed switches and routers interconnect different distribution layer switches, which in turn connect to access layer switches serving individual workstations, servers, and devices. SMB servers are commonly placed at the distribution or core layer to optimize access times for clients located across the campus. This structure allows for centralized file sharing via SMB, even when clients are geographically dispersed within the campus network.

In wide-area networks, where SMB must operate across greater distances between branch offices and data centers, hub-and-spoke topologies are frequently used. In this model, remote sites or branch offices (spokes) connect to a central headquarters or data center (hub). SMB traffic originating from remote offices is routed through the central hub, where the primary file servers and resources are hosted. While functional, this design can introduce latency and reduce performance, particularly over slower WAN links. To address these challenges, organizations may implement technologies like WAN optimization or deploy SMB file servers at branch locations to act as local caches for commonly accessed files, reducing the need to pull data from the central hub over the WAN repeatedly.

With the rise of hybrid cloud environments, SMB has also adapted to operate efficiently in topologies that integrate on-premises networks with public or private clouds. In these hybrid architectures, on-premises networks connect to cloud-based services via direct connections, VPNs, or secure internet links. SMB file shares hosted in the cloud, such as Azure Files or Amazon FSx, can be accessed by clients across the hybrid environment using secure, encrypted SMB sessions. These hybrid topologies allow organizations to maintain on-premises SMB infrastructure while extending file-sharing capabilities to remote users and cloud-hosted applications.

Another topology increasingly relevant to modern SMB deployments is the software-defined wide-area network (SD-WAN). SD-WAN topologies abstract the network underlay, dynamically routing SMB traffic over multiple transport services, such as MPLS, broadband internet, and LTE, based on real-time performance and policy considerations. This flexibility ensures that SMB traffic is delivered using the most efficient and reliable path, improving performance for remote users accessing centralized SMB file shares from branch offices or home networks.

Peer-to-peer (P2P) topologies, while less common in enterprise environments, also support SMB communications. In smaller office setups or temporary networks, SMB can function in an ad-hoc P2P topology, where clients directly share files with one another without the need for a centralized server. Although this approach can be convenient in small-scale scenarios, it lacks the centralized management, security controls, and scalability found in server-client SMB deployments within structured network topologies.

Virtualized environments introduce another layer of complexity to network topologies supporting SMB. In virtualized data centers, virtual switches and distributed virtual switches enable SMB traffic to flow between virtual machines (VMs) and storage systems without leaving the hypervisor host or data center network. SMB 3.x features such as SMB Direct and SMB Multichannel are leveraged to maximize performance in these environments, enabling hyper-converged infrastructures to efficiently share and access virtual machine disk files and other shared storage resources.

Regardless of the topology used, network administrators must consider factors such as bandwidth, latency, redundancy, and security when deploying SMB within their chosen network structure. Optimizing the underlying network design ensures that SMB's full potential is realized, enabling users to benefit from reliable, secure, and high-performance file-sharing capabilities. SMB's flexibility allows it to operate across a wide variety of network designs, from the simplicity of a local star topology to the complexity of a global hybrid-cloud mesh, making it an enduring and adaptable protocol in today's ever-evolving IT environments.

# Setting Up SMB on Windows Servers

Setting up SMB on Windows Servers is a fundamental task for system administrators looking to enable file and resource sharing within an organization. The process involves configuring the necessary roles and services on a Windows Server, creating and securing shared folders, and ensuring that the SMB protocol operates efficiently and securely within the network. Windows Server, as the primary platform supporting SMB in most enterprise environments, offers a range of tools and options that make deployment and management of SMB straightforward yet powerful.

The first step in setting up SMB on a Windows Server is to install the File and Storage Services role, which includes the necessary components to host SMB shares. On modern versions of Windows Server, such as Windows Server 2016, 2019, or 2022, this role is typically installed by default, but it can also be added via the Server Manager dashboard. Within Server Manager, administrators navigate to the Add Roles and Features wizard, select the File and Storage Services role, and ensure that subcomponents like the File Server role service are enabled. This prepares the server to create and manage shared folders and to handle incoming SMB requests from clients across the network.

Once the role is installed, the next step involves setting up one or more folders to be shared via SMB. This can be done through Server Manager, Windows Admin Center, or directly from File Explorer using the folder's properties menu. By right-clicking a folder and accessing its properties, administrators can open the Sharing tab and choose to share the folder over the network. The process allows for customization of the share name, which is the identifier clients will use to access the share via Universal Naming Convention paths such as \ServerName\ShareName. Proper naming conventions are important in larger networks to ensure clarity and organization, especially when managing dozens or hundreds of shares.

After defining the share, configuring the permissions is critical to maintaining security and proper access control. Windows Server allows administrators to set share permissions at two levels: the share level and the NTFS file system level. Share permissions control what actions network users can perform when accessing the share, typically allowing for read, change, or full control. NTFS permissions, meanwhile, offer more granular control by defining access at the file and folder level within the shared directory. Best practices dictate that administrators apply the principle of least privilege, granting users only the access necessary to perform their duties and minimizing the risk of accidental or malicious data alteration.

Advanced sharing options within the Windows Server environment also allow administrators to enable features such as access-based enumeration. When this option is activated, users will only see files and folders they have permissions to access, reducing clutter and improving security by preventing users from seeing sensitive directories to which they have no access rights. Additionally, administrators can configure offline files to allow certain users to cache copies of files locally on their devices, enabling them to continue working even when disconnected from the network.

Windows Server also provides tools for monitoring and auditing SMB shares. By configuring auditing policies through Group Policy or local security policies, administrators can track events such as file access, creation, deletion, and permission changes. This visibility is crucial for organizations that must comply with regulatory requirements or maintain strict internal controls over sensitive data. Logs generated by auditing can be reviewed using the Windows Event Viewer or forwarded to centralized security information and event management (SIEM) systems for further analysis and alerting.

Another important aspect of setting up SMB on Windows Server is ensuring that the correct version of the protocol is being used. Modern Windows Servers support SMB 3.1.1 by default, which includes advanced features such as pre-authentication integrity, AES-128-GCM encryption, and SMB Multichannel support. However, for compatibility reasons, some environments may need to support older SMB versions like SMB 2.x or, in rare legacy scenarios, SMB 1.0. Microsoft strongly advises disabling SMB 1.0 wherever possible due to its well-documented security vulnerabilities. Adjustments to SMB protocol settings can be made through PowerShell commands or Group Policy, allowing administrators to define which SMB versions are enabled on the server.

SMB encryption is another critical setting that can be configured on a per-share basis. When enabled, encryption ensures that data transmitted between clients and the SMB server is protected from interception and unauthorized access. Administrators can enable SMB encryption through PowerShell or within the advanced sharing settings in Server Manager. In environments where sensitive or regulated data is shared over SMB, encryption is a mandatory consideration to prevent exposure of confidential information.

Setting up SMB on Windows Server also involves consideration of network performance. Features like SMB Direct, which leverages RDMA-enabled network adapters, can significantly improve file transfer speeds and reduce CPU usage, especially in data-intensive environments like virtualization clusters or high-performance computing scenarios. SMB Multichannel further enhances performance by allowing multiple network interfaces to be used simultaneously, balancing traffic across available paths and providing redundancy in case of network adapter failure.

For larger organizations and enterprises, deploying SMB file shares in conjunction with Distributed File System (DFS) namespaces can improve both usability and resilience. DFS allows administrators to present multiple shared folders from different servers under a single unified namespace, simplifying access for users while enabling automatic referral and fault tolerance. This is particularly valuable in geographically distributed environments where file servers may be located in different regions but need to appear as a single, logical file structure to end-users.

Windows Server also integrates SMB file sharing capabilities with Active Directory, simplifying user authentication and access management. When clients access an SMB share, the server authenticates them using their domain credentials, allowing for seamless single sign-on experiences. This integration is critical for enforcing Group Policy Objects (GPOs) and centralized security policies across the network.

Finally, modern Windows Server platforms support SMB over QUIC, a feature that encapsulates SMB traffic within encrypted HTTP/3 connections. This is especially useful for mobile or remote workers who need secure access to file shares without relying on traditional VPNs, offering a faster and more resilient alternative that adapts well to modern hybrid work scenarios.

The process of setting up SMB on Windows Servers is a blend of straightforward configuration steps and more advanced tuning and security practices. From the initial role installation to the fine-tuning of permissions, encryption, and network performance features, SMB offers administrators a powerful and flexible solution for enabling file and resource sharing within a secure and efficient environment. Its seamless integration with Windows ecosystems, scalability for large enterprises, and adaptability to cloud and hybrid networks make SMB an essential tool in the deployment and management of modern IT infrastructures.

# SMB on Linux and Unix Systems

The integration of the Server Message Block (SMB) protocol into Linux and Unix systems has been pivotal in fostering interoperability between Windows-based environments and open-source platforms. While SMB originated within the Microsoft ecosystem, its widespread adoption across various industries led to a demand for non-Windows systems to communicate effectively using the same protocol. This requirement was addressed by the development of open-source implementations such as Samba, which has become the de facto standard for enabling SMB functionality on Linux and Unix systems.

Samba is an open-source software suite that provides seamless file and print services to SMB/CIFS clients. It allows Linux and Unix servers to share files, printers, and other resources with Windows clients as if they were native Windows servers. This capability is essential in mixed-OS environments, where both Windows and Linux/Unix machines coexist, often performing complementary roles within enterprise networks. The implementation of SMB via Samba allows administrators to consolidate file sharing, reduce redundancy, and improve operational efficiency by enabling cross-platform compatibility without requiring additional proprietary solutions.

The deployment of SMB services on Linux or Unix begins with the installation of the Samba package, which is readily available in the official repositories of most Linux distributions. Whether using Ubuntu, Debian, CentOS, Red Hat Enterprise Linux, or SUSE, administrators can install Samba using the system's package manager. Once installed, configuration revolves around the smb.conf file, typically located in the /etc/samba directory. This configuration file defines the server settings, global parameters, and individual share definitions that control how the Linux or Unix system presents its shared resources to SMB clients.

Within the smb.conf file, global settings dictate server behavior, such as the workgroup or domain it belongs to, logging preferences, security modes, and network interfaces on which the SMB service will listen for client connections. These settings are crucial for aligning the SMB server with the surrounding network infrastructure and ensuring compatibility with Windows clients that rely on specific workgroup or domain membership to locate available file shares.

Defining shared resources within smb.conf involves creating share definitions that specify the directory path being shared, access permissions, and options such as read-only or writable status. Administrators can also configure parameters to control how guest users are handled or enforce user-based authentication using Samba's integration with the underlying Linux user management system. Samba supports user-level security, whereby users are authenticated based on credentials stored in the local Linux system or via integration with external directory services such as LDAP or Microsoft Active Directory.

Samba's capability to integrate with Active Directory is one of its most powerful features, enabling Linux and Unix servers to act as native participants in Windows domains. By joining the Linux server to the domain using tools like realmd or winbind, Samba allows domain users to authenticate against Active Directory and access SMB shares based on their group memberships and associated access control policies. This integration streamlines user management and enforces centralized security practices across heterogeneous environments.

Beyond simple file sharing, Samba offers advanced functionality to support enterprise requirements. Features like Access Control Lists (ACLs) allow administrators to apply fine-grained permissions on shared files and directories, mirroring the flexibility of NTFS permissions on Windows servers. Samba also supports integration with Kerberos authentication, providing secure single sign-on experiences for domain-joined users. This tight coupling with enterprise authentication mechanisms ensures that Linux-based SMB shares adhere to the same security standards expected in Windows-based environments.

Performance optimization is another consideration when configuring SMB on Linux and Unix systems. Samba supports modern SMB dialects, including SMB 2.x and SMB 3.x, which introduce significant enhancements in terms of efficiency and security. By default, Samba will negotiate the highest SMB version supported by both the client and the server, but administrators can fine-tune the protocol version through smb.conf settings. Leveraging newer SMB versions unlocks features such as large MTU support, pipelining, and advanced caching mechanisms, which contribute to faster file transfers and reduced network latency.

Administrators deploying SMB on Linux servers often pair Samba with additional tools to enhance functionality and security. For example, integrating fail2ban can help protect Samba servers from brute force attacks by blocking repeated failed login attempts, while SELinux or AppArmor provides mandatory access controls to further restrict how Samba processes interact with the system. In clustered environments, Samba can be integrated with clustered file systems such as GlusterFS or CephFS, allowing for the creation of highly available and scalable SMB file shares capable of serving large, distributed user bases.

From a client perspective, Linux and Unix systems can also act as SMB clients by mounting SMB shares hosted on remote servers. This is typically achieved using tools like smbclient, which offers an FTP-like command-line interface for interacting with SMB shares, or by using mount.cifs to map SMB shares directly into the local file system hierarchy. By mounting remote SMB shares, Linux systems can seamlessly access Windows-hosted file shares, enabling users and applications to interact with remote files as if they were local.

The ability to both serve and consume SMB shares from Linux and Unix systems is crucial in industries where open-source technologies coexist with proprietary platforms. Environments such as academic institutions, media production houses, and research organizations frequently rely on Linux for its flexibility and cost-effectiveness, while still requiring interoperability with Windows systems used by other departments or business units. By enabling SMB on Linux and Unix, organizations can bridge the gap between these worlds, creating a unified file-sharing infrastructure that supports diverse workloads and user needs.

As SMB continues to evolve, so too does Samba. The project actively tracks and implements new SMB features, ensuring that Linux and Unix systems remain compatible with the latest Windows technologies and security enhancements. Ongoing developments include support for SMB 3.1.1 encryption, SMB Direct, and advanced auditing capabilities, bringing the open-source implementation closer to feature parity with Microsoft's native SMB offerings.

In summary, the implementation of SMB on Linux and Unix systems, primarily through Samba, enables robust and secure file sharing in mixed-OS environments. It allows open-source platforms to function as both servers and clients within SMB-based networks, providing the interoperability, flexibility, and performance required by modern organizations. From small businesses to global enterprises, the ability to leverage SMB on Linux and Unix has become a critical component of efficient and secure network file sharing.

# Cross-Platform File Sharing with SMB

Cross-platform file sharing has become an essential requirement for modern organizations operating in diverse IT environments where Windows, Linux, macOS, and other Unix-like systems coexist. The Server Message Block (SMB) protocol plays a pivotal role in bridging these disparate platforms by providing a common language for file and printer sharing. Originally developed for Windows, SMB has grown into a versatile protocol that enables seamless interaction across different operating systems, allowing users to share and access files regardless of the platform they are working on.

One of the key strengths of SMB in cross-platform file sharing is its ability to standardize communication between systems that inherently operate under different file system structures, authentication methods, and security models. In a typical enterprise network, Windows systems might rely on NTFS file systems and Active Directory for user authentication, while Linux and Unix servers operate with ext4 or XFS file systems and use local or LDAP-based authentication. macOS, on the other hand, uses APFS and integrates with Apple-centric directory services or can bind to Active Directory for larger enterprise deployments. Despite these architectural differences, SMB creates a unified interface that abstracts these distinctions, allowing users to map network drives, open files, and print to shared devices regardless of the operating system.

At the core of cross-platform file sharing with SMB is the Samba project, an open-source implementation that allows Linux and Unix systems to both host and access SMB shares. Samba enables Linux servers to provide SMB-based file shares that can be accessed by Windows and macOS clients using native file explorer interfaces, such as Windows Explorer or macOS Finder. This interoperability allows organizations to deploy file servers on cost-effective and flexible Linux platforms while still serving Windows desktops, laptops, and applications without the need for proprietary middleware or complex integration layers.

macOS, which is based on a Unix-like foundation, also includes native support for SMB, allowing Apple devices to participate fully in SMB-based file sharing networks. Apple transitioned to SMB as the default file-sharing protocol in macOS to improve compatibility with Windows networks and simplify the user experience in mixed-platform environments. macOS users can easily connect to SMB shares by entering the network path in Finder, browsing for available network shares, or using command-line utilities like mount_smbfs. This built-in SMB support ensures that macOS systems can integrate seamlessly into corporate networks dominated by Windows and Linux servers running SMB services.

SMB's role in cross-platform file sharing extends beyond basic file access to include printer sharing and inter-process communication. For example, a Linux server running Samba can present printers to Windows and macOS clients via SMB, allowing them to print directly to devices connected to the Linux system. In collaborative environments such as educational institutions, creative agencies, or research labs, this functionality enables users on different platforms to share common resources without encountering compatibility issues or requiring separate printer drivers for each operating system.

Security is a crucial factor when implementing cross-platform SMB file sharing. SMB leverages authentication mechanisms that can integrate with various identity management systems, such as Active Directory, LDAP, or local Unix user accounts. In mixed environments, Linux servers running Samba can join Windows Active Directory domains, allowing users to authenticate to SMB shares using their domain credentials. This integration provides a single sign-on experience, ensuring that users on Windows, Linux, and macOS systems can access shared files without the need for separate accounts or inconsistent security policies. For organizations implementing tighter security models, Samba supports Kerberos authentication, which aligns with enterprise best practices for secure network authentication and encrypted sessions.

Cross-platform file sharing with SMB also introduces challenges related to file system semantics. Windows, Linux, and macOS handle file permissions, case sensitivity, symbolic links, and extended attributes differently. SMB mediates these differences by translating or mapping certain file system features. For example, Linux systems with case-sensitive file systems may need special considerations when interacting with Windows clients that expect case-insensitive behavior. Administrators can configure Samba to enforce case-insensitive access, ensuring compatibility and reducing user confusion when navigating shared directories from different platforms.

Performance tuning plays an important role in cross-platform SMB deployments. Network latency, protocol version mismatches, and caching strategies all influence how well SMB functions across various systems. Modern SMB dialects, such as SMB 3.x, introduce features like large MTU support, opportunistic locking, and multichannel capabilities to improve file transfer speed and reduce latency, even when clients and servers are running different operating systems. Organizations can optimize performance by configuring clients to use the latest SMB versions supported by their operating systems and by fine-tuning Samba settings to align with workload requirements.

The ability of SMB to function across different types of networks further enhances its cross-platform versatility. Whether operating over local area networks (LANs), wide-area networks (WANs), or hybrid cloud environments, SMB adapts to support distributed teams and remote access scenarios. For example, macOS or Linux users can connect to SMB shares hosted on on-premises Windows servers or cloud-based storage solutions such as Azure Files or Amazon FSx, which natively support the SMB protocol. This allows organizations to extend their file-sharing capabilities to remote users without introducing new protocols or requiring changes to end-user workflows.

Cross-platform SMB file sharing is often complemented by additional services that help manage and secure file access. For instance, integrating SMB shares with centralized logging and monitoring tools provides visibility into user activities across all platforms. Administrators can track access patterns, detect unusual behavior, and ensure compliance with organizational policies regardless of whether the SMB client is a Windows workstation, a Linux development machine, or a macOS laptop.

The flexibility of SMB as a cross-platform protocol has contributed to its widespread adoption in industries such as education, healthcare, media production, and finance, where collaboration between users on multiple operating systems is common. In media production workflows, for example, designers and editors using macOS systems may need to access shared assets stored on Linux servers via SMB while simultaneously collaborating with project managers using Windows devices. This seamless interoperability ensures that projects can progress efficiently without requiring time-consuming file conversions or manual transfers between systems.

As networks continue to evolve, cross-platform SMB file sharing is increasingly extending into cloud-native environments. Modern organizations often deploy file shares in the cloud that are accessible to on-premises and remote systems alike. With cloud services offering SMB-compatible storage, organizations can leverage existing SMB-based workflows while adopting flexible, scalable storage solutions in the cloud.

The ability to unify file sharing across different operating systems with SMB reduces administrative complexity, enhances productivity, and ensures that users can focus on their tasks without being hindered by technical limitations. By providing a common protocol that supports Windows, Linux, Unix, and macOS, SMB remains a crucial element in facilitating collaboration and data access across today's multi-platform, distributed networks. Its cross-platform capabilities continue to enable organizations to create integrated, secure, and efficient file-sharing ecosystems that meet the needs of diverse and dynamic user bases.

# SMB Authentication Mechanisms

Authentication mechanisms are at the core of securing SMB communications within any networked environment. As the Server Message Block (SMB) protocol facilitates access to shared resources such as files, folders, and printers, it must enforce robust authentication methods to ensure that only authorized users gain access to these critical assets. Over the years, the SMB protocol has evolved to include multiple authentication techniques, ranging from basic password-based authentication to more advanced and secure mechanisms such as Kerberos. The choice of authentication method used within SMB sessions depends largely on the version of SMB being deployed, the operating systems involved, and the overarching security policies of the organization.

The earliest SMB implementations relied on simple challenge-response mechanisms, most notably the LAN Manager (LM) authentication protocol. LM authentication was developed in the 1980s as part of the original SMB 1.0 implementation. In LM authentication, when a client attempts to connect to an SMB server, the server generates a challenge string that is sent to the client. The client uses the user's password to encrypt this challenge and sends the result back to the server. The server then performs the same encryption and compares the results. If the two encrypted values match, authentication is successful. However, LM authentication has been proven to be highly insecure by modern standards due to its weak hashing algorithm, lack of support for long or complex passwords, and susceptibility to brute-force and rainbow table attacks.

To address the vulnerabilities of LM, Microsoft introduced NT LAN Manager (NTLM) authentication, which improved upon LM by using stronger cryptographic techniques. NTLM uses an MD4 hash of the user's password to generate the response to the server's challenge, offering a modest increase in security over LM. NTLM became the standard authentication method in SMB implementations during the 1990s, particularly in Windows NT environments. Despite its improvements, NTLM still suffers from several inherent weaknesses, including susceptibility to pass-the-hash attacks and vulnerability to relay attacks where attackers intercept and replay authentication requests to gain unauthorized access.

As security threats became more sophisticated and networks grew larger and more interconnected, it became necessary to adopt stronger and more scalable authentication methods. The introduction of Kerberos authentication into the Windows ecosystem marked a significant milestone in SMB security. Kerberos, a network authentication protocol developed by MIT, is based on trusted third-party authentication using a system of tickets issued by a Key Distribution Center (KDC). In environments integrated with Active Directory, Kerberos has become the default authentication method for SMB sessions starting with Windows 2000.

When SMB leverages Kerberos, a client authenticates to the KDC to receive a Ticket Granting Ticket (TGT). This ticket can then be used to request Service Tickets for specific services, such as accessing SMB shares on a file server. The file server, acting as the SMB service provider, accepts the Kerberos Service Ticket as proof of the client's identity. Kerberos eliminates the need to send password hashes over the network, mitigating the risk of interception and replay attacks. Additionally, Kerberos supports mutual authentication, ensuring that both the client and server verify each other's identities before any sensitive data is exchanged.

Beyond Kerberos and NTLM, modern SMB implementations, such as SMB 3.0 and SMB 3.1.1, include additional security features that complement the core authentication mechanisms. SMB 3.1.1

introduced pre-authentication integrity checks that help protect against man-in-the-middle attacks by verifying the integrity of the SMB session's initial handshake process. This integrity check ensures that attackers cannot tamper with the negotiation phase to downgrade the security capabilities of the SMB session, such as forcing it to use weaker authentication methods or disabling encryption.

SMB also supports authentication mechanisms that leverage external identity providers and federation services. For example, in hybrid environments where on-premises Active Directory is federated with cloud-based identity services like Azure Active Directory, users can authenticate to SMB shares hosted on Azure Files using their cloud credentials. This seamless authentication process allows organizations to unify their identity management across on-premises and cloud environments while enforcing modern security standards such as multifactor authentication and conditional access policies.

In Linux and Unix environments, Samba plays a crucial role in supporting SMB authentication. Samba can be configured to authenticate users through local Unix accounts, LDAP directories, or by integrating with Active Directory via Kerberos. When configured for Active Directory integration, Samba allows Linux file servers to become full-fledged domain members, providing SMB shares secured by the same Kerberos tickets used within the Windows ecosystem. This ensures that cross-platform SMB file sharing maintains a consistent and secure authentication experience for users, regardless of whether they access shares from Windows, Linux, or macOS clients.

Guest access represents another form of SMB authentication, though it is typically discouraged in secure environments. In guest access configurations, SMB shares are made available to unauthenticated users, granting access without requiring credentials. While this setup might be convenient for public or non-sensitive file shares in small office or lab environments, it introduces significant security risks in enterprise or regulated settings. SMB guest access is often disabled by default on modern Windows and Samba installations to prevent unauthorized access to shared resources.

The ongoing evolution of SMB has led to an increasing emphasis on encrypted communication in conjunction with strong authentication.

SMB encryption, available since SMB 3.0, provides end-to-end encryption of SMB traffic, protecting data even after successful authentication. While encryption does not replace authentication, it reinforces the security model by preventing eavesdropping and data tampering during file transfers and remote access sessions.

Modern best practices for SMB authentication recommend prioritizing Kerberos over NTLM whenever possible, disabling legacy protocols like LM, and enforcing encryption on all SMB communications. Administrators are encouraged to leverage tools like Group Policy Objects (GPOs) in Windows environments to enforce these security settings across all domain-joined systems. Additionally, organizations often implement security policies that require complex passwords, regular credential rotations, and multifactor authentication to further strengthen the protection of SMB sessions.

In high-security environments, SMB authentication is frequently supplemented with network access control mechanisms, firewall rules, and intrusion detection systems. By restricting which devices can initiate SMB sessions, monitoring for unusual authentication patterns, and applying zero-trust principles, organizations can create a layered defense that significantly reduces the risk of unauthorized access to SMB shares.

SMB's authentication mechanisms have matured significantly, evolving from basic challenge-response models to enterprise-grade, ticket-based systems. The combination of Kerberos, encryption, and integrity verification in modern SMB implementations ensures that organizations can maintain secure and efficient file-sharing operations even as network threats continue to grow in sophistication. As the backbone for secure file and resource access in countless organizations, SMB's authentication mechanisms remain critical to protecting data and upholding trust within modern network infrastructures.

# Understanding SMB Sessions and Connections

An essential part of comprehending how the Server Message Block (SMB) protocol functions within a networked environment is understanding the relationship between SMB sessions and connections. These two fundamental elements are at the heart of how SMB facilitates communication between clients and servers for the purpose of sharing files, printers, and other network resources. While often used interchangeably in casual conversation, sessions and connections serve distinct roles in the SMB architecture and impact how performance, security, and reliability are achieved.

An SMB connection refers to the underlying TCP connection established between an SMB client and an SMB server. This connection typically occurs over TCP port 445, though older implementations might also utilize NetBIOS over TCP/IP via port 139. The SMB client initiates the connection by sending a request to the server's SMB service, signaling the desire to begin communication. Once the TCP three-way handshake is completed, the client can initiate the SMB protocol negotiation to determine the dialect or version of SMB that will be used for the session. The connection itself provides the foundation on which one or multiple SMB sessions may be established.

A session, in contrast, is an authenticated context layered on top of the established SMB connection. The session represents the individual identity and authorization of a user or application interacting with the SMB server. During session setup, the client presents authentication credentials to the server, which can be verified via various methods such as NTLM or Kerberos, depending on the network's security configuration. Once authenticated, the session is created, and an associated session ID is generated to manage that session's context for the duration of the communication.

One key characteristic of SMB is that a single TCP connection may carry multiple SMB sessions concurrently. This feature enables multiple users or processes on the same client machine to establish independent sessions over a shared connection. For example, in a terminal server environment where multiple users are logged into a single Windows server, each user may establish an individual SMB session to access network shares, all running over the same underlying TCP connection between the server and the file share host. This multiplexing ability contributes to SMB's efficiency and scalability, particularly in environments with high user concurrency.

Once a session is established, the client may proceed to perform a wide array of SMB operations, including tree connect requests, which mount specific shared resources available on the server. The concept of a "tree" in SMB terminology refers to a share or resource such as a file share or printer. A successful tree connect operation allows the client to interact with the shared resource, performing tasks such as reading, writing, creating, or deleting files and directories. Each tree connect is associated with a session and is governed by the permissions and access controls applied to that session's credentials.

During the lifespan of a session, the SMB client sends a series of protocol messages, each formatted as SMB commands, to the server. These commands may involve file-level actions such as open, close, read, and write operations or control actions like locking files, querying directory contents, or retrieving file metadata. The session manages the context for these actions, ensuring that the permissions, state information, and security settings for the authenticated user or application are properly enforced throughout the exchange.

SMB sessions are designed to be persistent, meaning that they remain active until explicitly terminated by the client, disconnected due to inactivity, or interrupted by network failures. In scenarios where network disruptions are common, such as wide-area networks or unreliable wireless environments, modern SMB versions like SMB 3.x introduce mechanisms such as persistent handles. Persistent handles allow SMB sessions to resume interrupted file operations without requiring users to reopen files or restart applications, significantly improving resilience and user experience in unstable network conditions.

Another important feature related to SMB sessions is session signing, which provides message integrity verification. When session signing is enabled, each SMB message exchanged between the client and server is cryptographically signed to ensure that the message has not been altered in transit. Session signing is particularly valuable in environments where data integrity is critical, and it helps defend against man-in-the-middle attacks that could tamper with SMB messages. While session signing introduces additional overhead, modern networks typically have sufficient bandwidth and processing power to accommodate this added layer of security without negatively impacting performance.

Encryption further enhances the security of SMB sessions. SMB 3.0 and later versions support session-level encryption, which encrypts the entire SMB payload after authentication, ensuring that all file operations, metadata exchanges, and data transfers are protected from eavesdropping and interception. SMB encryption is negotiated as part of the session setup process and can be configured globally or on a per-share basis, depending on organizational policies and the sensitivity of the data being transmitted.

Understanding SMB connections also involves recognizing the role of SMB Multichannel, introduced in SMB 3.0. SMB Multichannel allows multiple network interfaces on the client and server to be utilized simultaneously within a single connection. This provides load balancing and failover capabilities, increasing throughput and ensuring redundancy in case one network path fails. Although SMB Multichannel operates at the connection level, the sessions that run on top of these connections benefit from the improved performance and resilience without requiring application-level modifications.

In virtualized or clustered environments, where servers may host hundreds or thousands of SMB sessions concurrently, efficient management of sessions and connections is vital. Administrators must ensure that server resources such as memory, CPU, and network bandwidth are sufficient to handle the volume of simultaneous sessions without degradation of performance. Monitoring tools provided by operating systems or third-party platforms can track active SMB connections and sessions, helping administrators identify bottlenecks or potential security threats, such as an unusually high number of failed session authentication attempts.

The termination of SMB sessions and connections is just as important as their establishment. Sessions can be closed manually by the client when access to shared resources is no longer needed or automatically by the server after periods of inactivity, depending on timeout policies. Likewise, connections may be dropped if network conditions degrade or if administrators explicitly close idle connections to conserve resources. Proper session and connection management is essential to maintaining the overall health and security of the SMB infrastructure.

The interaction between sessions and connections within the SMB protocol is a well-orchestrated process designed to optimize performance, enforce security, and ensure that users experience reliable and seamless access to shared network resources. By understanding how these components operate independently and together, IT professionals can better design, manage, and secure SMB-based environments, ensuring that both the technical and business needs of their organizations are consistently met.

# The CIFS Legacy in SMB

The Common Internet File System, more commonly known as CIFS, is an integral part of the historical narrative of the Server Message Block (SMB) protocol. For many years, CIFS was often used synonymously with SMB, though technically it refers to a specific dialect of the SMB protocol. Developed and popularized by Microsoft, CIFS emerged during the 1990s as an extension and formalization of the earlier SMB protocol created by IBM. As Microsoft integrated SMB into its Windows NT line of products, the company began using the term CIFS to describe its proprietary implementation of SMB 1.0 with additional extensions intended to improve compatibility and support over modern network environments of the time.

CIFS played a crucial role in establishing SMB as the dominant file-sharing protocol within enterprise environments, especially those built around Windows operating systems. Its design was centered on providing users with seamless access to remote files and printers, allowing them to open, edit, and manage resources over a network as if they were local. CIFS was designed to work over the TCP/IP protocol suite, a significant shift from earlier SMB implementations that often relied on NetBIOS over IPX/SPX or NetBEUI, which were more prevalent in legacy systems.

One of the defining characteristics of CIFS was its orientation toward Internet and WAN usage, aiming to provide file-sharing capabilities beyond local area networks. To achieve this, CIFS introduced extensions that allowed it to better handle larger file sizes and longer filenames in alignment with modern file system standards such as NTFS. The protocol also incorporated enhanced session management features, more robust locking mechanisms to avoid data corruption during concurrent file access, and improved error-handling routines that allowed clients and servers to recover more gracefully from network interruptions.

However, while CIFS advanced the capabilities of SMB in significant ways, it also carried with it several inefficiencies and limitations that became more apparent as networking technology evolved. CIFS used a highly verbose communication model, with each action—such as opening a file, reading data, or writing to a file—resulting in numerous individual request-response cycles between the client and server. This chatter-heavy nature made CIFS less efficient over high-latency networks, such as WANs or early internet connections, where the delay between each roundtrip could significantly degrade performance.

CIFS also lacked native encryption and relied on older, less secure authentication mechanisms, such as LAN Manager (LM) and NT LAN Manager (NTLM), which have since been deprecated due to vulnerabilities that could be exploited by attackers. The absence of end-to-end encryption and modern cryptographic protections made CIFS traffic particularly vulnerable to eavesdropping, man-in-the-middle attacks, and session hijacking when used over untrusted networks. These limitations became increasingly problematic as enterprises connected to the broader internet and adopted remote access models that demanded higher security standards.

Despite these shortcomings, CIFS became a de facto standard during the late 1990s and early 2000s, supported not only by Windows systems but also by Unix and Linux machines through the use of the open-source Samba project. Samba implemented CIFS support to allow Unix-like systems to interact seamlessly with Windows file shares, creating the cross-platform interoperability that many businesses required. CIFS also saw adoption in various embedded systems and network-attached storage (NAS) devices, further solidifying its role in networked file sharing during that period.

The legacy of CIFS continued to shape the development of SMB long after its initial release. As Microsoft continued to enhance the SMB protocol to meet the demands of modern IT environments, many of the fundamental concepts introduced with CIFS—such as universal file sharing across diverse network types—remained foundational. However, CIFS itself, as a dialect, became increasingly obsolete with the introduction of SMB 2.0 and subsequent versions.

SMB 2.0, released with Windows Vista and Windows Server 2008, addressed many of the inefficiencies and security weaknesses associated with CIFS. It reduced the number of commands used in file operations, introduced pipelining and compounding to allow multiple actions to be bundled into single requests, and significantly decreased the overhead that plagued CIFS communications. Additionally, SMB 2.0 improved file and directory caching, reduced the amount of unnecessary metadata retrieval, and provided much-needed performance enhancements for networks with higher latency.

As SMB 3.0 and later versions introduced features such as end-to-end encryption, SMB Multichannel for load balancing across network interfaces, and SMB Direct for RDMA-enabled high-speed data transfers, CIFS was gradually phased out. Microsoft and other industry leaders began recommending the disabling of CIFS and SMB 1.0 entirely, particularly following several high-profile cybersecurity incidents, such as the WannaCry ransomware attack, which exploited vulnerabilities in legacy SMB 1.0/CIFS deployments.

Despite its retirement in most modern systems, CIFS left a lasting imprint on file-sharing protocols and network communication models. Many network administrators and IT professionals still colloquially refer to SMB shares as CIFS shares, a testament to how deeply ingrained CIFS became in the collective vocabulary of enterprise IT environments. In documentation, configurations, and common usage, the term CIFS often lingers even as organizations have moved to more secure and efficient SMB versions.

Today, CIFS is largely considered a legacy protocol, retained only in specific niche environments where legacy systems or applications require backward compatibility. Modern best practices recommend disabling SMB 1.0/CIFS on servers and clients unless absolutely necessary, opting instead for newer SMB versions that provide superior security, efficiency, and scalability. Most contemporary operating systems, including recent Windows, Linux, and macOS releases, default to using SMB 2.x or SMB 3.x dialects for file-sharing operations.

While CIFS is no longer recommended for active use, understanding its legacy is crucial for IT professionals tasked with maintaining, migrating, or decommissioning legacy infrastructures. The transition from CIFS to modern SMB dialects highlights the broader narrative of how file-sharing protocols have adapted to meet the rising expectations of security, performance, and interoperability in the digital age. CIFS serves as both a historical milestone in the evolution of networked file systems and a reminder of the ongoing need to modernize and secure critical IT infrastructure. Its legacy continues to inform the design and implementation of current and future iterations of SMB, shaping how file sharing is conceptualized and executed across networks today.

# SMB and Active Directory Integration

The integration of the Server Message Block (SMB) protocol with Active Directory (AD) represents one of the most critical elements in modern enterprise networks. SMB provides the means for clients to access shared resources such as files, folders, and printers over a network, while Active Directory provides centralized authentication, authorization, and directory services for users, groups, and computers within a Windows domain. The combination of these two technologies creates a powerful framework for secure and efficient resource sharing across organizations of all sizes. This integration is not only a technical necessity but also a foundational component in implementing security best practices, enforcing corporate policies, and streamlining administrative tasks.

At the core of SMB and Active Directory integration is the concept of centralized identity management. Active Directory maintains a database of user accounts, computer objects, security groups, and organizational units that represent the logical structure of an organization's IT environment. By authenticating SMB sessions using credentials stored in Active Directory, organizations can ensure that access to shared resources is consistently and securely controlled. This eliminates the need for local user accounts on each SMB server, reducing administrative overhead and enabling single sign-on (SSO) experiences for end-users.

When a client initiates an SMB session to access a shared resource hosted on a server joined to an Active Directory domain, the authentication process leverages either NTLM or, preferably, Kerberos. Kerberos, as the default authentication mechanism in Active Directory-integrated environments, offers robust security through the use of ticket-granting services provided by the domain's Key Distribution Center (KDC). This system ensures that both the SMB client and server trust the same authority, the domain controller, which issues the necessary tickets to verify identity. Kerberos enables mutual authentication, meaning that not only does the server validate the client's credentials, but the client also verifies the server's identity, protecting against man-in-the-middle attacks.

SMB shares hosted on servers joined to Active Directory domains benefit from fine-grained access control through Access Control Lists (ACLs) and share permissions that are directly tied to AD users and groups. For example, administrators can configure an SMB share to grant read-only access to the "Finance" security group while allowing full control for the "Finance Managers" group. These permissions are centrally managed within Active Directory, ensuring that changes to group memberships or user accounts are automatically reflected in the access rights enforced on SMB shares. This integration streamlines user and permissions management, making it easy for IT teams to onboard new employees, apply role-based access controls, and comply with internal or external regulatory requirements.

In addition to file and folder permissions, SMB integrates with Active Directory Group Policy Objects (GPOs) to enforce broader network policies. GPOs can be used to configure client-side SMB settings, such as requiring SMB signing for message integrity or enabling SMB encryption to secure data in transit. Administrators can also define policies for offline file availability, user profile redirection, and network drive mapping through logon scripts or Group Policy Preferences. This allows for automated configuration of SMB client settings across all domain-joined machines, ensuring consistency and reducing the likelihood of misconfigurations that could expose security vulnerabilities or impact productivity.

The integration between SMB and Active Directory extends to auditing and logging, which are essential components of a secure and well-managed network. When users authenticate to SMB shares using their domain credentials, these actions are recorded and can be reviewed using tools like Windows Event Viewer, Advanced Security Audit Policies, or centralized Security Information and Event Management (SIEM) platforms. Audit logs can provide detailed information on who accessed which files, at what time, and from which machine, enabling organizations to detect suspicious activities, investigate incidents, and maintain compliance with industry regulations such as GDPR, HIPAA, or PCI-DSS.

In environments where Linux or Unix systems are present, Samba provides the means for non-Windows servers to fully integrate with Active Directory and participate in SMB resource sharing. By configuring Samba to join an Active Directory domain, Linux servers can act as SMB file servers that authenticate users against Active Directory, enforce AD-based access controls, and support Kerberos authentication. This enables seamless interoperability between Linux and Windows systems within the same SMB and Active Directory ecosystem, allowing organizations to benefit from cross-platform file sharing without sacrificing centralized management or security.

Advanced SMB features also take advantage of Active Directory integration to enhance performance and reliability. For instance, Distributed File System (DFS) namespaces, often deployed alongside SMB shares, are managed through Active Directory. DFS namespaces create a unified directory structure that abstracts multiple SMB shares across different servers into a single logical namespace. Active Directory stores the DFS configuration, which clients use to locate the nearest or most available SMB server hosting the requested resource.

This not only simplifies the user experience but also enables load balancing and fault tolerance for critical file shares.

Active Directory integration with SMB is also essential in supporting modern authentication and access models, such as those found in hybrid and cloud environments. With the rise of Azure Active Directory and hybrid identity solutions, SMB can leverage cloud-based authentication for users accessing SMB shares hosted in cloud services like Azure Files. This allows organizations to extend their on-premises Active Directory infrastructure into the cloud, providing users with secure access to SMB resources from virtually anywhere while maintaining a unified identity management strategy.

Security remains a paramount consideration in SMB and Active Directory integration. Administrators are encouraged to enforce the use of modern SMB versions, disable legacy protocols like SMB 1.0, and configure SMB signing and encryption to prevent tampering and eavesdropping on sensitive data. Active Directory's granular control over password policies, account lockout thresholds, and multifactor authentication can further enhance the protection of SMB-based resource access. When combined with firewalls, network segmentation, and intrusion detection systems, SMB and Active Directory integration form a comprehensive defense-in-depth strategy.

The integration between SMB and Active Directory has become a cornerstone of enterprise networking, offering a scalable, secure, and highly manageable solution for file and resource sharing. By centralizing user authentication, enforcing consistent access controls, and supporting advanced security measures, this integration reduces complexity and strengthens organizational security postures. It enables businesses to manage vast and distributed IT infrastructures with efficiency, ensuring that users across departments, locations, and even different operating systems can securely and reliably access the resources they need. As organizations continue to evolve and adopt hybrid IT models, the enduring relationship between SMB and Active Directory remains fundamental to their operational success.

# Managing SMB Shares and Permissions

Effectively managing SMB shares and permissions is crucial for any organization that relies on network-based file sharing to support its operations. SMB, as a protocol, enables the distribution and centralized access of files, folders, and printers, but without proper share configuration and permission management, organizations risk exposing sensitive data, creating operational inefficiencies, and complicating the user experience. The process of managing SMB shares and permissions involves the careful creation, configuration, and maintenance of shared resources, combined with the application of security principles to regulate who can access what, and at what level.

At the most basic level, creating an SMB share begins with selecting a folder or directory on the server to be shared across the network. This share becomes a network-accessible resource that clients can connect to using UNC paths, typically formatted as \ServerName\ShareName. Whether implemented on a Windows Server, a Linux machine running Samba, or another SMB-compatible platform, administrators must balance ease of access with security controls. The naming conventions used for shares should follow consistent and descriptive patterns to help users easily identify available resources and prevent confusion in large environments where multiple shares might exist for different teams, projects, or departments.

Once an SMB share has been created, managing permissions becomes the next critical step. Permissions can be divided into two categories: share-level permissions and file system-level permissions. Share-level permissions are applied at the network share itself, determining what remote users or groups can do when connecting to the share. These typically include permissions such as read, change, or full control. Read allows users to view and open files but not make modifications. Change includes the ability to create, delete, or modify files and folders, while full control grants complete administrative rights over the shared resource, including the ability to modify permissions themselves.

In parallel, file system-level permissions are applied directly to the files and folders within the shared directory using the file system's native access control mechanisms. On Windows servers, this is typically handled via NTFS permissions, while on Linux systems running Samba, it may involve POSIX file permissions or Access Control Lists (ACLs). NTFS permissions allow administrators to apply much more granular access rights, such as limiting user access to specific subfolders or individual files within a share. This layered approach allows organizations to enforce broad access restrictions at the share level and apply more detailed rules within the share to regulate specific user or group actions.

A best practice in SMB share management is to align permissions with the principle of least privilege, meaning users are only granted the minimum level of access necessary to perform their job functions. This reduces the risk of accidental file deletion or unauthorized data modification. For instance, a financial reports folder might be shared with a finance group having change access, while other employees may only be granted read access to view finalized reports. Administrators should regularly review and audit these permissions to ensure they reflect current organizational roles and responsibilities, particularly after staffing changes or project transitions.

Role-based access control (RBAC) is commonly used to simplify SMB share management. Instead of assigning permissions directly to individual users, permissions are assigned to security groups within Active Directory or local user groups on non-domain systems. Users are then placed into the appropriate groups according to their roles. This allows for easier management of permissions, as modifying access for multiple users simply involves adding or removing them from the designated groups. It also makes auditing simpler, as group memberships can be reviewed and validated against organizational policies.

Managing SMB shares and permissions also involves configuring advanced features designed to improve security and user experience. One such feature is access-based enumeration (ABE), which controls the visibility of files and folders within a share. When enabled, ABE ensures that users can only see files and folders for which they have permission, reducing unnecessary clutter and preventing users from seeing restricted directories. This is particularly valuable in environments with shared folders that house both public and confidential subfolders, ensuring sensitive data remains hidden from unauthorized users.

Offline files represent another important capability, allowing SMB shares to be synchronized locally to client devices. When configured correctly, offline files enable users to continue accessing and editing files from SMB shares even when disconnected from the network. Once connectivity is restored, changes are synchronized back to the server. Administrators can control which shares allow offline file caching and apply Group Policy settings to automate synchronization behavior and storage limits.

In highly secure environments, administrators may also enforce SMB signing and encryption on shares. SMB signing ensures that all communications between client and server are verified for integrity, preventing man-in-the-middle attacks where data could be intercepted and altered. Encryption, available in SMB 3.0 and later, secures SMB traffic over the network, protecting sensitive data from eavesdropping. These settings can be enforced on a per-share basis or globally across the SMB service.

Proper management also requires monitoring and auditing SMB shares. File access auditing can be configured to track events such as successful or failed file access attempts, file modifications, deletions, and permission changes. These logs, captured via Windows Event Viewer or forwarded to centralized logging systems, provide crucial insights into user behavior, helping to identify potential misuse, policy violations, or security incidents. Periodic reviews of these logs are essential for maintaining a secure and compliant file-sharing environment.

Samba, the most common SMB implementation on Linux and Unix systems, offers similar flexibility in managing shares and permissions. Samba's smb.conf file allows administrators to define each share, set guest or authenticated access policies, and integrate with Active Directory for centralized user authentication. File-level permissions on Samba shares can be managed using POSIX permissions or extended ACLs, offering comparable control to NTFS. Samba also supports features such as VFS (Virtual File System) modules that can introduce additional functionality like recycle bin integration or quota enforcement within SMB shares.

In distributed or enterprise environments, SMB shares are often integrated with Distributed File System (DFS) namespaces, simplifying access to shares spread across multiple servers by presenting them under a single logical path. This further improves manageability by centralizing access points while allowing backend file shares to be distributed for load balancing and redundancy purposes.

Ultimately, managing SMB shares and permissions requires a combination of technical knowledge, security awareness, and proactive maintenance. It is not only about enabling users to access shared resources but also about ensuring that this access is structured, controlled, and aligned with the organization's operational and security needs. When done effectively, it enhances productivity, protects sensitive information, and creates a streamlined and secure file-sharing environment capable of supporting the demands of modern business operations.

# Access Control Lists (ACLs) in SMB

Access Control Lists, commonly referred to as ACLs, play a vital role in securing resources and managing permissions within the Server Message Block (SMB) protocol. SMB facilitates the sharing of files, folders, and printers over a network, but without proper access controls, these shared resources could be easily exploited or misused. ACLs enable administrators to define precisely who can access specific objects and what actions they are permitted to perform. By applying ACLs to SMB shares and the underlying file system, organizations can implement a robust and granular security model that aligns with their operational needs and regulatory requirements.

An ACL is essentially a list of rules or entries attached to an object such as a file, folder, or printer. Each entry in this list, known as an Access Control Entry (ACE), specifies permissions for a particular user or group. In the context of SMB, ACLs typically govern actions like reading files, writing data, modifying content, deleting resources, or changing permissions. The flexibility of ACLs is one of their key strengths, as they allow administrators to define detailed and specific access rights for different users and groups, going beyond the simplistic read/write/execute model found in basic permission systems.

Within a Windows environment, ACLs are implemented through the NTFS file system, which is fully integrated with SMB. When a user attempts to access an SMB share, the file system's ACLs are consulted to determine if the requested action is permitted. This system of layered security means that even if a share-level permission grants general access to a shared folder, the NTFS ACLs can further restrict or refine what users can do once inside that folder. For example, an SMB share may be configured to allow access to all members of a department, but the ACL might limit write access to a subset of users who are project leads.

An ACL contains multiple ACEs, each defining permissions for a specific user, security group, or even a built-in system account such as SYSTEM or Everyone. Each ACE defines the scope of allowed or denied actions for the subject. Permissions in an ACL can be either explicit, where a rule directly defines an action, or inherited, where permissions flow from parent objects, such as a folder's permissions applying to its subfolders and files unless overridden. This inheritance model simplifies the management of large directory structures by reducing the need to set permissions individually on every single object.

Permissions within ACLs can be broken down into standard and advanced types. Standard permissions include common actions such as read, write, and full control. Advanced permissions offer finer granularity, allowing control over specific actions like reading file attributes, creating folders, deleting subfolders, or taking ownership of an object. This level of detail is essential in complex environments where responsibilities are divided among multiple users, and it is necessary to precisely define who can modify or manage certain files.

SMB, when used in conjunction with Active Directory, leverages ACLs to enforce access based on centralized security groups and user accounts. This ensures consistency across the network, as permissions defined through ACLs automatically apply to any user or group authenticated by Active Directory. For example, a financial reports folder might be accessible only to users in the Finance security group, while the HR department's documents may be restricted exclusively to members of the HR group. By managing these groups in Active Directory and applying corresponding ACEs within the ACLs, administrators maintain control over sensitive data and reduce the risk of unauthorized access.

An important feature of ACLs is their ability to explicitly deny permissions, overriding any allowed permissions that might otherwise be granted through group memberships or inheritance. This deny mechanism provides an essential tool for administrators who need to create exceptions to general access rules. For instance, while a marketing folder might be accessible to all members of the marketing department, a specific subfolder containing confidential campaign strategies might have a deny ACE applied to block access for certain junior staff members.

On Linux and Unix systems using Samba to provide SMB services, ACLs can also be enforced using POSIX ACLs or Extended ACLs, depending on the file system in use. These ACLs function similarly to NTFS ACLs, allowing administrators to define access rights beyond the traditional owner-group-other model. Samba integrates with these native ACL mechanisms, ensuring that ACLs applied at the file system level are honored when users connect to Samba shares over SMB. This compatibility enables organizations to maintain fine-grained access controls even in cross-platform environments where Linux and Windows servers coexist.

Managing ACLs effectively requires a combination of technical precision and organizational insight. Administrators must understand the organizational structure, job roles, and data sensitivity to apply ACLs that protect data without hindering productivity. Misconfigured ACLs can result in either overly permissive access, where sensitive files are exposed to unauthorized users, or overly restrictive settings that disrupt workflows and delay projects. Regular audits of ACL configurations are necessary to identify outdated or misaligned permissions and to ensure compliance with internal security policies or external regulatory standards.

Advanced tools and interfaces assist in managing ACLs within SMB environments. On Windows servers, administrators can use the graphical user interface available through the Properties > Security tab of a file or folder to view and modify ACLs. More complex scenarios, such as bulk permission changes or automated permission audits, may leverage PowerShell scripts or command-line tools like icacls. These tools enable administrators to apply or review ACLs across large sets of files and directories, ensuring consistency and efficiency.

Monitoring the effectiveness of ACLs also involves auditing user activity related to SMB shares. By enabling file system auditing through Group Policy or local security policies, administrators can log events such as successful or failed access attempts, permission changes, and object deletions. This audit trail can then be analyzed to detect unusual patterns, such as unauthorized access attempts or privilege escalations, providing valuable insights for security teams.

In modern SMB environments, ACLs are a critical component of a broader security strategy. When combined with SMB encryption, session signing, firewall policies, and secure authentication methods like Kerberos, ACLs help establish a multilayered defense that protects data while supporting efficient and collaborative workflows. Their flexibility and granularity make them indispensable for organizations seeking to secure sensitive information and manage access rights in a scalable and maintainable way. By mastering the deployment and maintenance of ACLs within SMB shares, administrators ensure that their networked resources are both accessible to authorized users and protected from potential threats.

# SMB and Group Policy Management

The integration of SMB with Group Policy Management is a crucial aspect of centralized control in Windows-based enterprise networks. Group Policy provides administrators with a powerful tool to enforce system and security settings, manage configurations, and streamline operational tasks across hundreds or even thousands of computers in a domain. When combined with SMB, Group Policy Management allows organizations to automate and secure file sharing, enforce access restrictions, and ensure that SMB-related settings are consistently applied across all domain-joined devices. This integration plays a central role in defining how users interact with network resources, how permissions are distributed, and how secure communication is maintained in SMB-based environments.

At its core, Group Policy allows administrators to define a set of rules and settings within Group Policy Objects (GPOs) that are applied to users and computers within Active Directory. These policies control various system behaviors, including how SMB operates on client and server systems. One of the most common uses of Group Policy with SMB is the deployment of mapped network drives. By using Group Policy Preferences, administrators can automatically map SMB shares to specific drive letters on user workstations. This eliminates the need for manual mapping by users and ensures that each employee has immediate access to the required shared folders when logging into the domain. Network drives mapped through Group Policy can be tailored to user roles by leveraging security group filtering, ensuring that only users in specific departments or teams receive certain drive mappings.

Beyond drive mapping, Group Policy also plays a key role in defining the security settings of SMB communication. Administrators can use Group Policy to enforce SMB signing, which ensures that all SMB traffic is signed to verify message integrity. Enabling SMB signing prevents attackers from altering SMB packets in transit, a critical protection against man-in-the-middle attacks. Group Policy settings related to SMB signing can be found under the Computer Configuration > Policies > Windows Settings > Security Settings > Local Policies > Security Options section, where options to digitally sign SMB communications (always or when possible) can be configured for both client and server roles.

Another important SMB-related configuration available through Group Policy is SMB encryption. Starting with SMB 3.0, SMB supports end-to-end encryption, securing data in transit between clients and servers without the need for additional VPN tunnels. Group Policy can enforce encryption for SMB shares by defining policies that require encrypted SMB sessions. This is particularly useful in environments where sensitive data is accessed over less secure or remote networks, such as between branch offices or over wireless connections. By mandating encryption via Group Policy, administrators ensure that all SMB traffic is automatically protected against interception.

Group Policy is also instrumental in controlling SMB protocol versions allowed within an organization. SMB 1.0, being an outdated and vulnerable protocol, is often disabled as part of a secure baseline policy. Using Group Policy, administrators can configure domain-joined systems to disable SMB 1.0 client and server components while ensuring that only secure versions, such as SMB 2.0 and SMB 3.x, are enabled. This helps mitigate the risk of exploitation through vulnerabilities associated with older SMB versions, such as those leveraged in the infamous WannaCry ransomware attack.

Another powerful use of Group Policy with SMB involves the control of offline files and caching behavior. Offline files allow users to continue accessing SMB share data even when disconnected from the network. Group Policy can be used to configure which SMB shares allow offline file caching and how that caching is managed on client devices. Administrators can enable or disable caching, control synchronization schedules, and set disk space limits, optimizing how offline files function according to network conditions and user needs.

In highly secure environments, Group Policy can be used to implement granular user rights assignments related to SMB access. For instance, administrators can define who is allowed to access the server from the network, who is permitted to manage file shares, and who has the ability to back up or restore files. These rights directly impact how users and administrators interact with SMB shares and are essential for establishing a secure operational model that aligns with the principle of least privilege.

Auditing policies related to SMB activity can also be configured through Group Policy. By enabling auditing of object access or logon events, administrators can collect valuable data about how SMB shares are being used. For example, audit logs can reveal which users are accessing specific files, when files are being modified or deleted, and whether there are repeated failed access attempts. Group Policy ensures that auditing is consistently enforced across all applicable systems, supporting forensic investigations and compliance reporting requirements.

For organizations utilizing Distributed File System (DFS) namespaces in conjunction with SMB shares, Group Policy can manage referral ordering and namespace access permissions. DFS allows administrators to consolidate multiple SMB shares into a unified namespace, simplifying resource access for end users. Group Policy can dictate how DFS referrals are presented to clients, such as prioritizing referrals to local or high-availability servers based on network site awareness. This enhances the user experience by improving access speeds and resilience when connecting to shared resources.

In environments where SMB is deployed alongside other Microsoft technologies, such as Remote Desktop Services (RDS) or virtual desktop infrastructure (VDI), Group Policy allows for further customization of SMB behaviors. Policies can be applied to manage SMB client-side caching, limit the maximum number of simultaneous SMB client sessions, or define session timeouts, helping to optimize performance and resource utilization in multi-user or virtualized scenarios.

Group Policy also streamlines the deployment of security hardening templates that include recommended SMB configurations as part of broader system baselines. For example, organizations may apply CIS Benchmarks or Microsoft Security Compliance Toolkit settings via Group Policy to enforce secure SMB settings across all endpoints. These predefined templates provide an easy way to ensure that SMB-related security best practices are consistently implemented throughout the organization.

By leveraging Group Policy to manage SMB settings, administrators gain centralized control, improve efficiency, and reduce the risk of misconfigurations that could compromise security or affect user productivity. Group Policy ensures that all domain-joined computers adhere to the organization's file-sharing policies, reducing the manual overhead of configuring each system individually and ensuring a uniform user experience across the network. The relationship between SMB and Group Policy Management is a prime example of how centralized configuration management tools can enhance the security, stability, and efficiency of enterprise IT environments. SMB's flexibility combined with the power of Group Policy allows administrators to build secure, scalable, and easy-to-manage file-sharing infrastructures that support diverse operational needs.

# Auditing SMB File Access

Auditing SMB file access is a vital process for organizations aiming to maintain control over their data, ensure regulatory compliance, and enhance security within their networks. The Server Message Block protocol provides a mechanism for users to share and access files over a network, but without adequate monitoring and auditing in place, organizations risk losing visibility into how these shared resources are being used. SMB file access auditing allows administrators to track who is accessing files, what actions they are taking, and when these activities occur. This level of insight is essential not only for detecting unauthorized or malicious activity but also for troubleshooting operational issues and satisfying auditing requirements mandated by industry regulations.

The foundation of SMB file access auditing lies in configuring the appropriate auditing policies on the file server where the SMB shares are hosted. On Windows Server, this process typically begins by enabling object access auditing via Group Policy or local security policies. Object access auditing focuses on tracking interactions with file system objects, such as files and folders, and generates security events whenever configured criteria are met. Administrators can enable this setting under the Local Policies section of the Security Options within Group Policy Management or via the Local Security Policy snap-in on individual servers.

Once object access auditing is enabled at the policy level, administrators must specify which files or folders to audit and what types of access attempts to track. This is done by modifying the Advanced Security Settings of the shared folders and configuring the Auditing tab. Here, specific users, groups, or even system accounts can be selected, and administrators can choose to log events such as read access, write operations, file deletions, permission changes, or failed access attempts. By applying auditing selectively, organizations can focus on monitoring sensitive or high-value directories without generating excessive logs that could overwhelm storage or make incident investigation more complex.

Auditing SMB file access generates entries in the Windows Security Event Log, which can be accessed through the Event Viewer utility. Each event contains detailed information, including the user account involved, the source computer's IP address, the action taken, the time of the event, and whether the attempt succeeded or failed. Event IDs, such as 4663, are commonly associated with file access auditing and help administrators filter and categorize logs. By reviewing these logs regularly, IT and security teams can identify patterns indicative of unauthorized activity, such as repeated failed attempts to open confidential files or unusual file access during non-business hours.

In enterprise environments, where SMB shares are accessed by hundreds or thousands of users, manual log review is impractical. To address this, many organizations forward SMB audit logs to centralized Security Information and Event Management (SIEM) platforms. SIEM solutions collect, normalize, and correlate log data from multiple servers, providing real-time monitoring, alerting, and advanced analytics. By setting up alerts for suspicious behavior, such as bulk file deletions or access attempts from unusual geographic locations, administrators can respond quickly to potential security incidents.

Auditing SMB file access also plays a critical role in meeting compliance obligations for standards like the General Data Protection Regulation (GDPR), the Health Insurance Portability and Accountability Act (HIPAA), and the Payment Card Industry Data Security Standard (PCI DSS). These regulations often require organizations to maintain detailed records of who has accessed sensitive data and to ensure that only authorized personnel can interact with protected information. Comprehensive SMB file access logs provide an auditable trail that demonstrates adherence to these requirements and can be presented during internal or external audits.

Another benefit of auditing SMB file access is its ability to help organizations investigate and resolve operational issues. For example, when a file is accidentally deleted or modified, administrators can review audit logs to determine who performed the action and under what circumstances. This forensic capability reduces downtime by quickly identifying the root cause of data loss or unauthorized modifications, allowing teams to take corrective actions, such as restoring files from backup or adjusting permissions to prevent recurrence.

In addition to auditing user interactions, organizations may also choose to audit administrative actions taken on SMB shares themselves. This includes tracking changes to share permissions, monitoring who creates or deletes shares, and logging when key settings are modified. By auditing administrative activities, organizations protect against insider threats and ensure that all configuration changes are properly documented and reviewed.

For Linux and Unix environments running Samba, file access auditing can also be enabled, although the process differs from native Windows implementations. Samba supports integration with syslog and can be configured to log file access events for shares served via SMB. Administrators can modify the smb.conf configuration file to enable logging of successful and failed file operations, specifying the desired log level and directing logs to a centralized logging system for further analysis. While Samba's built-in auditing features may not provide the same granularity as Windows auditing, third-party tools or integration with audit frameworks such as auditd can extend capabilities in Linux environments.

A well-structured SMB file access auditing strategy requires careful planning to strike a balance between visibility and manageability. Excessive auditing can generate an overwhelming volume of data, consuming system resources and storage. To avoid this, administrators should prioritize auditing on sensitive folders, such as those containing financial records, intellectual property, or personally identifiable information (PII). They should also establish data retention policies that define how long audit logs are stored based on regulatory requirements and business needs.

Automation plays a vital role in modern auditing practices. Many organizations use scripts or SIEM integrations to automate log collection, analysis, and reporting. Automated alerts can notify administrators in real-time if unusual activities, such as mass file movements or privilege escalations, are detected. Dashboards and periodic reports generated from audit logs provide valuable insights into user behavior, helping teams improve data governance and identify potential risks.

Auditing SMB file access is not solely a security measure; it also supports broader business objectives. By monitoring how data is accessed and used across departments, organizations can make informed decisions about resource allocation, storage optimization, and data lifecycle management. Usage patterns revealed through audit logs may indicate that certain shares are underutilized and could be archived, or that specific data sets are accessed frequently and may benefit from improved storage performance.

Ultimately, auditing SMB file access strengthens an organization's ability to protect critical information assets, comply with industry regulations, and support business continuity. It provides the transparency necessary to manage data responsibly in a connected and collaborative environment, ensuring that file-sharing activities are both secure and accountable across the enterprise.

# SMB Encryption: SMB 3.x and Beyond

SMB encryption has become a critical component of securing data in modern network environments. With the introduction of SMB 3.0 and subsequent versions, Microsoft significantly enhanced the security posture of the SMB protocol by incorporating native encryption mechanisms. Prior to SMB 3.0, securing SMB traffic largely depended on external technologies such as IPsec or virtual private networks, which added complexity and required separate configuration and management. SMB 3.x marked a turning point by embedding encryption directly into the protocol, offering protection for data in transit between SMB clients and servers without the need for additional layers.

The need for SMB encryption became increasingly evident as organizations expanded their networks beyond traditional local area networks and into distributed environments that included remote offices, mobile users, and hybrid cloud deployments. As sensitive data traversed more varied and less trusted networks, the risk of interception and unauthorized access grew. Early SMB implementations, including SMB 1.0 and SMB 2.x, did not include built-in encryption, leaving organizations reliant on other network security solutions to safeguard SMB traffic. SMB signing, introduced earlier, provided integrity checking but did not encrypt the data payloads themselves. This left critical gaps, especially in scenarios where files containing intellectual property, financial records, or personally identifiable information were being accessed across unsecured or public networks.

With the release of SMB 3.0 in Windows 8 and Windows Server 2012, Microsoft introduced end-to-end encryption at the transport layer, offering a simple and effective method to secure SMB traffic. This encryption capability is negotiated during the SMB session setup phase and is applied transparently to all file operations, directory queries, and metadata exchanges between clients and servers. The encryption process ensures that SMB traffic is unreadable to unauthorized parties, even if captured by attackers through packet sniffing or other interception techniques.

SMB 3.0 encryption utilizes the Advanced Encryption Standard (AES) algorithm with 128-bit keys operating in CCM (Counter with CBC-MAC) mode. This encryption standard was chosen for its balance of security and performance, providing strong protection without significantly impacting network throughput or CPU utilization. By securing SMB traffic natively, organizations gained the ability to protect sensitive data on internal corporate networks, across data center interconnects, and even over WAN links without relying on external VPN tunnels.

Subsequent versions of SMB further refined and improved the encryption feature set. SMB 3.1.1, released with Windows 10 and Windows Server 2016, introduced support for AES-128-GCM (Galois/Counter Mode), which provides enhanced security and improved performance compared to AES-128-CCM. AES-GCM is widely regarded as a modern, high-performance encryption standard that integrates both encryption and integrity checking in a single step, reducing overhead and accelerating cryptographic operations. SMB 3.1.1 also introduced pre-authentication integrity checks using SHA-

512, designed to protect the SMB handshake process itself from tampering and downgrade attacks.

One of the key advantages of SMB encryption is its flexibility. Administrators can configure encryption globally at the server level or selectively enable it on individual SMB shares. This allows organizations to apply encryption where it is most needed based on sensitivity or compliance requirements while minimizing resource consumption on less critical or internal-only shares. On Windows Server systems, administrators can enable SMB encryption through PowerShell commands, the Server Manager interface, or via Group Policy settings, making it easy to deploy across large environments.

Another important benefit of SMB encryption is that it operates independently of the underlying network. Unlike VPNs, which require additional network infrastructure and may introduce routing complexity or latency, SMB encryption works seamlessly over any IP-based network. Whether users are accessing files on-premises, from a branch office, or from the cloud, encryption is automatically applied as long as both the client and server support the feature and it has been configured appropriately.

Performance considerations are always a factor when deploying encryption at scale. While early concerns existed regarding the potential overhead of encrypting large volumes of file system traffic, improvements in hardware and software optimization have largely addressed these concerns. Modern processors offer hardware acceleration for AES encryption, reducing the CPU load on both clients and servers during encrypted SMB sessions. Additionally, the introduction of SMB Multichannel allows organizations to leverage multiple network interfaces simultaneously, distributing the encrypted traffic across available links and mitigating performance bottlenecks.

SMB encryption also plays a significant role in securing hybrid cloud and remote work environments. As more organizations migrate workloads to cloud platforms such as Microsoft Azure, services like Azure Files have adopted SMB 3.x encryption to protect data in transit between Azure storage accounts and client devices. This allows enterprises to extend their existing SMB-based workflows into the cloud while maintaining compliance with data protection regulations that require encryption of sensitive information over untrusted networks.

Administrators should also be aware of compatibility considerations when implementing SMB encryption. Both the SMB client and server must support at least SMB 3.0 for encryption to be negotiated successfully. In mixed environments where legacy systems still rely on SMB 2.x or SMB 1.0, encryption will not be available, highlighting the importance of modernizing legacy infrastructure. Microsoft strongly recommends disabling SMB 1.0 wherever possible due to its lack of encryption and other critical security shortcomings.

For Linux and Unix environments that utilize Samba to provide SMB services, encryption support has also been incorporated in recent versions. Samba, beginning with version 4.1, introduced support for SMB 3.x encryption, allowing Linux servers to offer secure SMB shares to Windows clients. Administrators can configure Samba's smb.conf file to require encryption on specific shares or enable it globally, ensuring that traffic is protected across heterogeneous networks. This advancement has been essential for organizations running mixed-OS environments, where interoperability and security must coexist.

Beyond file sharing, SMB encryption extends to other SMB-based services such as printing and named pipes, further broadening its protective scope. In scenarios where applications rely on SMB for remote procedure calls or interprocess communication, encryption ensures that sensitive data exchanged within these workflows is shielded from interception.

The evolution of SMB encryption reflects the broader shift toward building secure-by-design protocols that meet the demands of modern, distributed computing. As remote access, cloud integration, and hybrid work models become the norm, encrypting data in transit is no longer optional but a fundamental security requirement. SMB encryption, introduced in SMB 3.0 and refined in SMB 3.1.1, provides organizations with the tools to meet this challenge without sacrificing the usability and performance that SMB has long been known for.

The ability to enforce encryption policies through Group Policy or PowerShell scripting simplifies deployment and ensures consistency across the organization. As a result, SMB encryption remains a cornerstone of secure file sharing and resource access, enabling businesses to operate confidently in today's complex and interconnected IT landscape. The continual development of SMB beyond version 3.x promises further advancements, such as encryption tied to modern transport layers like QUIC, which will further enhance performance and security in future SMB implementations.

# SMB Signing for Data Integrity

SMB signing is a critical security mechanism designed to ensure the integrity of SMB communications between clients and servers across a network. By validating the authenticity of each SMB message, signing helps protect against tampering and interception, ensuring that the data exchanged in SMB sessions has not been altered in transit. In environments where sensitive information is shared, SMB signing adds an essential layer of protection, safeguarding users and systems from man-in-the-middle (MITM) attacks and session hijacking attempts. Although signing does not encrypt the actual data being transmitted, it guarantees that messages have not been modified or forged, playing a vital role in securing enterprise file sharing.

SMB signing was first introduced in SMB 1.0 and has been continually improved in subsequent SMB protocol versions. The fundamental concept behind SMB signing is straightforward. Each SMB message is signed using a cryptographic hash function that generates a unique signature based on the message content and a session key shared between the client and server. When the server receives a signed message from the client, it uses the session key to recalculate the hash and compares it with the signature sent by the client. If both values match, the message is verified as authentic and unaltered. If the values differ, the message is rejected, and the session can be terminated to prevent further exploitation.

The session key used for signing is derived from the authentication phase of the SMB session, which typically relies on NTLM or Kerberos. When using Kerberos, the session key is obtained from the Key Distribution Center, enhancing security by tying the integrity of SMB messages to the organization's centralized authentication system. This process ensures that only parties with valid authentication credentials can establish signed SMB sessions.

SMB signing is particularly important in networks where SMB traffic crosses multiple segments, including unsecured or semi-trusted networks. Without signing, attackers positioned between the client and server could intercept SMB packets and manipulate their contents, potentially injecting malicious commands or altering file contents during transfer. With signing enabled, such tampering is immediately detected, as the cryptographic signature would no longer match the recalculated value on the receiving end.

Administrators can configure SMB signing through Group Policy, local security policies, or directly via registry settings. In a domain environment, Group Policy provides a centralized method to enforce signing requirements across all domain-joined systems. Policies can be applied to require signing for SMB client communications, server communications, or both. This ensures that all SMB sessions initiated or accepted by compliant devices include cryptographic message integrity verification, regardless of user configuration or application behavior.

SMB signing policies offer flexibility in how they are enforced. Signing can be configured as "enabled," meaning it will be used if supported by both the client and server, or "required," which mandates that all SMB sessions must be signed or they will fail to establish. The latter setting is often recommended in high-security environments where data integrity is paramount, and the risk of MITM attacks is elevated, such as in financial institutions, government agencies, or networks handling classified information.

One consideration when implementing SMB signing is the potential impact on performance. The process of generating and verifying cryptographic hashes for each SMB message introduces additional CPU overhead and can slightly reduce throughput in high-traffic environments. However, modern hardware with cryptographic acceleration capabilities, as well as optimizations introduced in later SMB versions, have minimized this impact for most workloads. Organizations must weigh the benefits of enhanced security against potential performance trade-offs, although in many cases, the decrease in performance is negligible compared to the protection gained.

With the advent of SMB 2.0 and later versions, SMB signing became more efficient and scalable. SMB 2.x and SMB 3.x streamline the signing process by reducing the number of required message exchanges and optimizing how signatures are applied to larger or compounded SMB requests. These improvements, combined with better caching and pipelining, ensure that signing can be enforced without significantly hindering user experience or application responsiveness.

In SMB 3.1.1, released with Windows 10 and Windows Server 2016, Microsoft introduced pre-authentication integrity, which complements SMB signing by adding integrity checks during the session negotiation phase itself. Pre-authentication integrity uses the SHA-512 hashing algorithm to verify the handshake process, ensuring that attackers cannot manipulate the negotiation of SMB features, such as forcing the downgrade of a session to weaker security settings. This step further secures the integrity of SMB sessions from their very inception, closing gaps that could be exploited before message signing takes effect.

SMB signing can also be used in conjunction with other security technologies to provide a defense-in-depth approach. When combined with SMB encryption, introduced in SMB 3.0, signing adds an extra layer of protection by verifying message integrity in addition to encrypting the payload. In environments where data confidentiality is as important as integrity, using both signing and encryption is a recommended best practice. While encryption ensures that data cannot be read by unauthorized parties, signing ensures that even encrypted data has not been altered or tampered with.

From a compliance perspective, SMB signing helps organizations meet regulatory and security framework requirements that mandate integrity controls for data in transit. Frameworks such as NIST SP 800-53, ISO/IEC 27001, and CIS benchmarks all emphasize the importance of securing communications between networked systems. By enabling SMB signing, organizations demonstrate that they are taking proactive steps to protect the integrity of sensitive data, supporting auditability and compliance verification efforts.

In cross-platform environments, SMB signing remains relevant. Linux and Unix systems running Samba can also support SMB signing when interacting with Windows systems. Samba allows administrators to enable signing via the smb.conf file, offering compatibility with Windows clients that require signed SMB sessions. This ensures that file sharing across heterogeneous networks maintains a consistent level of integrity protection, regardless of the underlying operating system.

Operational best practices recommend conducting regular audits of SMB signing configurations across the network to ensure that all critical systems comply with the organization's security policies. Tools such as PowerShell can be used to query the signing status of SMB connections, while vulnerability scanners and configuration management tools can flag systems where signing is disabled or not enforced. Remediation steps may include updating Group Policy settings, patching outdated systems, and educating users on secure file-sharing practices.

SMB signing remains a foundational security feature in protecting data integrity across networked environments. While newer SMB versions have introduced additional enhancements, the core value of SMB signing persists. It provides organizations with a practical and effective way to defend against manipulation of SMB communications and plays a vital role in strengthening trust within distributed IT infrastructures. As businesses continue to rely on SMB for critical file sharing, printer access, and remote resource management, maintaining the integrity of these sessions through SMB signing is a necessary and prudent security measure.

# Common SMB Vulnerabilities

The Server Message Block protocol, while essential for network file sharing and resource access, has historically been a frequent target for attackers due to its widespread deployment and the sensitive data it often transports. Over the years, several SMB vulnerabilities have been identified that threaten the security, integrity, and availability of networked systems. Understanding these common vulnerabilities is crucial for IT and security professionals tasked with protecting enterprise environments where SMB plays a key role.

One of the most notorious vulnerabilities is associated with SMB version 1.0, which is now considered a legacy protocol. SMBv1, introduced in the 1980s, lacks modern security mechanisms such as encryption, strong authentication, and proper message integrity checks. These deficiencies have made it a prime target for attackers. The vulnerability exploited by the EternalBlue exploit, which leveraged a flaw in SMBv1 to execute arbitrary code on target machines, was used in the devastating WannaCry ransomware attack in 2017. WannaCry spread rapidly by using EternalBlue to propagate across networks, encrypting data and demanding ransom payments from victims. The underlying flaw exploited by EternalBlue was due to improper handling of specially crafted SMB packets, allowing remote code execution with system-level privileges. Despite widespread awareness of this flaw, some organizations still run legacy systems that require SMBv1, putting them at continued risk.

Another common vulnerability stems from the use of weak authentication mechanisms. Older SMB versions support NTLM and, in some cases, even the outdated LAN Manager (LM) authentication protocol. Both LM and NTLM have well-known weaknesses, including susceptibility to brute-force attacks and pass-the-hash techniques, where attackers can capture password hashes from SMB sessions and reuse them to authenticate without needing to crack the password itself. SMB sessions that are not signed are also vulnerable to man-in-the-middle attacks, where an adversary intercepts and modifies SMB traffic between the client and server without detection. Without SMB signing or encryption, the attacker could inject malicious commands or exfiltrate sensitive data.

SMB is also prone to exploitation through information disclosure vulnerabilities. Misconfigured SMB shares, commonly referred to as open shares, expose files and directories to unauthorized users when access controls are not properly applied. Publicly accessible shares without proper authentication controls may allow attackers to browse sensitive directory structures, download confidential documents, or gain further insight into the network topology. Open shares are frequently discovered in network audits, and in environments where Active Directory integration is not used or improperly configured, access to these shares may be available to any unauthenticated network user.

Another SMB vulnerability comes from a lack of access control and insufficient segmentation of the network. SMB services exposed to external or untrusted networks are particularly vulnerable, as attackers can directly probe for SMB servers and attempt to exploit known flaws or brute-force credentials. Misconfigured firewalls that expose port 445 (used by SMB) to the internet or external environments create an easily exploitable attack surface. Numerous ransomware campaigns have scanned the internet for exposed SMB services, exploiting weak configurations to initiate attacks.

Denial of service (DoS) vulnerabilities are another persistent issue within SMB implementations. Attackers can exploit flaws in SMB's handling of malformed packets to crash the SMB service or the underlying operating system itself. For instance, sending a series of crafted SMB packets designed to exhaust system resources or trigger buffer overflows can disrupt file sharing services and cause downtime, impacting business continuity. These types of attacks are particularly damaging in environments where SMB plays a critical role in delivering applications, documents, and collaboration tools to users.

Another common risk associated with SMB is the presence of unpatched systems running outdated versions of Windows or Samba. Many SMB vulnerabilities have been publicly disclosed and patched by vendors, but organizations often face challenges in deploying updates due to operational constraints, legacy applications, or lack of awareness. Attackers commonly exploit these gaps by using automated tools to identify vulnerable systems and apply known exploits, including those targeting outdated SMB services.

Credential relay attacks, such as the SMB relay attack, exploit the lack of mutual authentication in some SMB configurations. In this scenario, an attacker intercepts a legitimate authentication attempt from a user or system and relays the credentials to another SMB server to gain unauthorized access. This attack can be used to pivot across network segments, escalate privileges, or access sensitive shares. While SMB signing and mutual authentication via Kerberos can mitigate this risk, environments that rely solely on NTLM without signing remain vulnerable.

Another vulnerability often overlooked is related to the default configurations of SMB servers. Default shares such as ADMIN$, IPC$, and C$ are administrative shares automatically created by Windows systems. While these shares are typically restricted to administrative accounts, if compromised credentials are used in combination with open administrative shares, attackers can gain full control over a system, deploy malware, or exfiltrate data. Organizations that fail to secure administrative shares or apply proper network segmentation can unknowingly expose critical systems to lateral movement by attackers.

Even with modern SMB versions such as SMB 3.x, misconfiguration can still introduce vulnerabilities. Administrators may deploy SMB 3.x but fail to enforce encryption or signing, leaving SMB traffic unprotected from eavesdropping and tampering. Additionally, SMB shares that do not follow the principle of least privilege, where users are granted excessive permissions, are vulnerable to internal threats. Insider attackers or compromised accounts could delete, modify, or steal sensitive data if access controls are not properly configured.

Finally, the rise of hybrid cloud environments introduces new challenges for SMB security. Exposing SMB shares to cloud environments without proper security measures can introduce vulnerabilities associated with internet-facing file services. Cloud-based SMB services such as Azure Files offer encryption and advanced security features, but if improperly configured, organizations may unintentionally create shares accessible to unauthorized users over public networks.

Addressing these common SMB vulnerabilities requires a multi-layered approach to security. Disabling outdated SMB versions such as SMBv1, enforcing SMB signing and encryption, regularly auditing share permissions, applying security patches promptly, and implementing network segmentation are critical steps. Organizations must also ensure that firewall rules block SMB traffic from crossing security boundaries where unnecessary and that exposed services are monitored for suspicious activity. By understanding and mitigating these vulnerabilities, businesses can protect themselves against a broad range of cyber threats that continue to target SMB as a primary vector for attack.

# SMB and Ransomware Attacks

The Server Message Block protocol, while fundamental for network file sharing, has been repeatedly exploited in ransomware attacks, making it a key target in cybercrime campaigns around the world. SMB's role in facilitating the exchange of files, printer access, and remote resource management across enterprise environments has also made it a pathway for attackers seeking to infiltrate networks, encrypt valuable data, and demand ransom payments from their victims. As ransomware has evolved into a highly profitable criminal industry, SMB has frequently been at the center of large-scale incidents that have disrupted businesses, hospitals, governments, and critical infrastructure.

The most infamous example of SMB being used in ransomware attacks is the global WannaCry outbreak of 2017. WannaCry leveraged the EternalBlue exploit, which targeted a critical vulnerability in the SMBv1 implementation on unpatched Windows systems. By sending specially crafted SMB packets, attackers were able to trigger remote code execution on vulnerable machines, allowing them to deploy ransomware without user interaction. Once inside a network, WannaCry propagated automatically by scanning for other SMBv1-enabled systems, exploiting them to spread laterally and encrypt files across entire organizations. This worm-like behavior, made possible by SMB's role in connecting networked devices, allowed WannaCry to cause massive disruption in a matter of hours, locking down hospitals, transportation systems, and corporations worldwide.

Ransomware operators continue to favor SMB as an attack vector because of its deep integration into business workflows. Many organizations maintain extensive SMB share infrastructures to facilitate collaboration among employees, departments, and branches. This reliance on SMB creates an ideal opportunity for attackers. Once inside a network, often via phishing emails or compromised remote access tools, attackers can leverage SMB to move laterally, identify critical file shares, and deploy ransomware payloads to multiple machines and servers. The ability to target shared folders containing sensitive documents, customer data, and project files amplifies the impact of the attack, increasing the pressure on victims to pay the demanded ransom.

One common tactic in modern ransomware campaigns is the manual exploitation of SMB shares. Attackers may compromise an endpoint through other means and then scan the internal network for accessible SMB shares. Misconfigured shares that lack proper access controls or are open to all authenticated users are often targeted first. Files within these shares can be encrypted directly, or ransomware binaries can be staged onto servers and executed to cause widespread encryption of the server's contents and client-accessible directories. Attackers frequently escalate privileges by harvesting administrative credentials and using them to deploy ransomware across all reachable SMB shares, maximizing damage.

Advanced ransomware groups have also been observed combining SMB exploitation with credential dumping techniques. Tools like Mimikatz are used to extract cached credentials from compromised machines, which are then used to authenticate to additional SMB shares. By chaining together these tactics, attackers can compromise entire domains and gain access to backup repositories, financial data, and other mission-critical files stored on SMB servers. This lateral movement across SMB infrastructure allows ransomware actors to extend their reach beyond initial points of entry and cause organization-wide disruption.

Beyond encryption, some ransomware operations now employ double extortion tactics. In addition to encrypting data stored on SMB shares, attackers exfiltrate copies of sensitive information, threatening to publish or sell the data if the ransom is not paid. SMB's role in providing centralized file access means that attackers often find valuable data in shared folders, including customer records, contracts, and intellectual property. These files are typically easy to access if the organization has weak permission structures or relies on legacy SMB implementations without modern security controls.

The vulnerabilities in older SMB versions, particularly SMBv1, continue to present opportunities for ransomware attacks. Despite repeated warnings and industry guidance recommending the decommissioning of SMBv1, some organizations still maintain legacy systems or devices that require the outdated protocol. This creates an ongoing risk, as attackers actively scan networks for SMBv1 services exposed to the internet or internal networks. Once detected, these services can be quickly exploited, often resulting in ransomware deployment within minutes of discovery.

Ransomware campaigns targeting SMB shares have also evolved to evade detection and maximize disruption. Some modern strains are designed to identify and encrypt files used by popular enterprise applications, such as databases and document management systems, which are commonly stored on SMB shares. In addition, ransomware payloads may include commands to disable or delete Windows Volume Shadow Copies, preventing victims from restoring data without external backups. By targeting SMB shares that house shared backups or redundant file storage, attackers further reduce the victim's ability to recover without paying the ransom.

Mitigating the risk of ransomware attacks that leverage SMB requires a multi-faceted approach to security. Disabling SMBv1 is a critical first step. SMBv2 and SMBv3, particularly with encryption and signing enabled, provide significantly improved defenses compared to their predecessor. Implementing strict access controls on SMB shares is equally important. The principle of least privilege should govern access to shared folders, ensuring that only authorized users can read, modify, or execute files, and that administrative shares are secured against unauthorized access.

Network segmentation is another essential defense mechanism. By isolating critical servers and SMB shares from the broader user network, organizations can limit the ability of ransomware to propagate laterally. Firewalls should restrict SMB traffic between network segments where appropriate, and port 445 should never be exposed to the internet unless absolutely necessary and properly secured.

Continuous monitoring and auditing of SMB share activity can help detect ransomware behavior in its early stages. Unusual patterns, such as mass file modifications or deletions within short timeframes, can be indicative of ransomware in action. Security tools like endpoint detection and response (EDR) solutions and SIEM platforms can alert administrators to these anomalies, allowing them to respond swiftly to limit the spread of encryption.

Backups remain one of the most effective safeguards against the damage inflicted by SMB-enabled ransomware attacks. Regularly backing up data and storing copies offline or in isolated environments ensures that even if SMB shares are compromised, organizations can recover their data without paying a ransom. However, backup shares must be protected by strong access controls, as ransomware operators specifically seek out and destroy backup data stored on network-accessible SMB shares.

As ransomware continues to evolve, SMB will likely remain a favored vector due to its ubiquity and critical role in enterprise file sharing. Organizations must implement layered security controls around their SMB infrastructure, including patch management, protocol hardening, network segmentation, and continuous monitoring, to reduce their exposure to ransomware threats. Proactive defense strategies and a strong security culture are key to minimizing the likelihood of SMB-related ransomware incidents and ensuring business resilience in the face of this persistent and growing cyber threat.

# Securing SMB with Firewalls and VPNs

The Server Message Block protocol is a widely used method for file sharing, printer access, and remote management across local and wide-area networks. However, its openness and broad deployment make it a common target for attackers seeking to exploit misconfigurations and vulnerabilities. One of the most effective ways to reduce the attack surface of SMB services is through the strategic use of firewalls and virtual private networks. These tools play a crucial role in limiting SMB traffic exposure, enforcing access restrictions, and ensuring that SMB communications occur within secure, controlled network boundaries.

Firewalls serve as a first line of defense by regulating the flow of network traffic based on defined security policies. At their most basic level, firewalls can block or permit traffic to and from specific ports and IP addresses. For SMB, this typically involves controlling traffic over port 445, which is the default TCP port for SMB communication on modern networks. In older implementations, SMB also used port 139 for NetBIOS over TCP/IP. One of the foundational best practices in network security is to block SMB ports at the network perimeter firewall, preventing external entities from initiating SMB connections to internal servers and clients. Allowing SMB traffic to traverse directly from the internet into the internal network creates an unnecessary attack vector and exposes the organization to threats such as ransomware and remote code execution exploits.

Internal network firewalls can also play a key role in segmenting SMB traffic within the enterprise. Network segmentation involves dividing the internal network into zones based on trust levels, functions, or business units. By placing critical SMB servers, such as those hosting sensitive file shares, within isolated network segments, organizations can restrict SMB traffic to only trusted subnets or VLANs. This approach limits the lateral movement potential for malware or attackers who breach one part of the network, as they would be unable to access restricted SMB shares without navigating through additional layers of firewall controls.

In addition to perimeter and internal segmentation, host-based firewalls installed on servers and client machines provide an additional layer of protection. By configuring the Windows Defender Firewall or third-party host-based firewalls, administrators can limit SMB services to accept connections only from known and trusted IP ranges. For instance, a file server can be configured to accept SMB connections solely from the corporate LAN and management network while rejecting attempts from guest or external-facing networks. Host-based firewalls also offer granularity, allowing rules to be applied to individual SMB shares or services depending on business needs.

While firewalls help restrict where SMB traffic can originate and terminate, VPNs are used to secure how this traffic traverses untrusted networks. A virtual private network creates an encrypted tunnel between two points, typically between remote users or offices and the corporate network. By encrypting all traffic within this tunnel, VPNs protect SMB sessions from eavesdropping and man-in-the-middle attacks when SMB traffic passes over public infrastructure such as the internet. Without a VPN or another secure transport method, SMB traffic sent across public networks would be vulnerable to interception and tampering, especially if encryption is not enabled within the SMB protocol itself.

VPNs are essential in supporting remote work scenarios where employees need to access SMB shares from outside the corporate network. Instead of exposing file servers directly to the internet, organizations can require remote users to connect through a VPN to access internal resources securely. Once inside the VPN tunnel, users can map network drives, browse file shares, and access printers via SMB as if they were on the local corporate LAN. This approach maintains a secure perimeter while supporting flexibility and productivity for distributed teams.

Site-to-site VPNs further enhance SMB security for organizations with multiple physical locations. By establishing VPN tunnels between branch offices and the central data center, SMB traffic between locations is encrypted and isolated from the public internet. This ensures that sensitive data being transferred between offices is protected from interception and that SMB communications comply with internal security policies. Site-to-site VPNs also reduce the need for ad-hoc firewall exceptions, streamlining the management of cross-site file sharing.

Firewalls and VPNs also contribute to compliance with industry regulations and security frameworks. Standards such as PCI DSS, HIPAA, and ISO/IEC 27001 require organizations to protect sensitive data in transit and limit unnecessary exposure of services to external networks. By enforcing firewall rules that restrict SMB traffic and requiring VPNs for remote access, organizations meet these regulatory expectations while significantly lowering their cybersecurity risk profile.

In more advanced security architectures, organizations may choose to combine firewalls and VPNs with other protective technologies such as network access control, intrusion detection and prevention systems, and zero-trust network principles. Network access control solutions ensure that only compliant and authorized devices can establish VPN connections or communicate with internal SMB services. Intrusion detection systems can monitor SMB traffic within VPN tunnels for suspicious patterns, such as lateral movement behavior or brute-force login attempts against SMB servers. Integrating these technologies with firewall and VPN policies creates a robust multi-layered security model around SMB.

Another consideration when using VPNs to secure SMB traffic is performance. VPN encryption can introduce latency, especially when handling large file transfers common in SMB workflows. To address this, organizations may deploy VPN solutions that support hardware acceleration or use optimized protocols such as IPsec with AES encryption or newer protocols like WireGuard. Balancing security with performance is key to ensuring that users do not circumvent security controls due to degraded file access speeds.

Organizations should also ensure that firewall rules and VPN configurations are regularly reviewed and updated. As networks grow and change, outdated rules may leave unnecessary SMB ports exposed, or VPN tunnels may not include all required subnets. A regular audit of firewall policies ensures that only required SMB traffic is allowed and that obsolete or overly permissive rules are removed. Similarly, VPN configurations should be periodically reviewed to ensure that they are enforcing strong encryption standards and that user access controls remain aligned with business needs.

Training and awareness are complementary measures that enhance the effectiveness of firewalls and VPNs in securing SMB. Users must be educated on the importance of connecting through VPNs when accessing internal file shares remotely, and IT teams must remain vigilant in monitoring SMB traffic for potential abuse. Ensuring that all users understand proper VPN usage helps reduce the likelihood of data leakage and reinforces the organization's security culture.

Ultimately, combining the strengths of firewalls and VPNs creates a secure environment for SMB operations. Firewalls define and enforce the network boundaries through which SMB traffic can flow, while VPNs protect the confidentiality and integrity of that traffic when traversing untrusted networks. Together, these controls mitigate many of the risks associated with SMB services, including unauthorized access, eavesdropping, and exploitation of vulnerabilities. As cyber threats continue to evolve, implementing and maintaining a strong firewall and VPN strategy remains essential for protecting SMB infrastructure and securing business-critical data.

# SMB Hardening Best Practices

Hardening the Server Message Block protocol is a critical priority for any organization relying on SMB for file sharing, printer access, and remote resource management. SMB has long been a target for attackers due to its deep integration into business operations and its history of vulnerabilities. Implementing SMB hardening best practices reduces the risk of unauthorized access, data breaches, lateral movement, and ransomware attacks. A thorough hardening strategy focuses on disabling outdated protocol versions, strengthening authentication, limiting exposure, applying granular permissions, and implementing additional security controls to safeguard SMB services within a modern IT infrastructure.

One of the most important best practices is the complete removal of SMB version 1.0 from all systems. SMBv1 is an outdated protocol that lacks modern security features, such as encryption and message signing by default, making it vulnerable to exploits like EternalBlue. Organizations should disable SMBv1 across all servers, clients, and network appliances. Microsoft provides group policies and PowerShell commands to facilitate the deactivation of SMBv1 services, and most modern operating systems no longer install SMBv1 by default. Legacy systems requiring SMBv1 should be isolated from the rest of the network and scheduled for decommissioning as soon as possible.

Enforcing the use of SMBv2 or SMBv3 is the next step in hardening SMB infrastructure. These newer versions offer enhanced performance and security features, including support for SMB signing and encryption. Administrators should configure systems to only allow connections using these modern dialects. SMBv3, in particular, introduces critical improvements such as end-to-end encryption and multichannel support, reducing both security risks and network latency.

SMB signing should be enabled wherever feasible to protect against man-in-the-middle attacks. SMB signing ensures the integrity of SMB packets by appending a cryptographic signature to each message. This signature validates that the data has not been tampered with during transit. For organizations with high-security requirements, SMB signing can be enforced via group policy, ensuring that all SMB communications are signed and that unsigned sessions are rejected. In combination with SMB encryption, which is available starting with SMB 3.0, signing helps establish a secure and trustworthy communication channel between clients and servers.

Network exposure is another critical element to address. SMB should never be exposed directly to the public internet. Firewalls must be configured to block inbound traffic on port 445 from external networks, allowing SMB connections only within trusted internal networks or through secure tunnels like VPNs. Proper segmentation of internal networks limits the ability of attackers to move laterally using SMB if one part of the network is compromised. Critical SMB servers should reside in isolated segments, and access should be restricted to only the systems and users that require it.

Granular access control through permissions and group memberships is key to limiting unnecessary access to SMB shares. The principle of least privilege should guide how shares are configured, ensuring users and groups have only the rights needed for their specific roles. Administrators should avoid using overly permissive settings such as granting full control to "Everyone" or "Authenticated Users" and should instead assign rights to specific security groups aligned with business roles. Additionally, administrators must ensure that sensitive shares, especially those containing personal data or proprietary information, are hidden from unauthorized users by using access-based enumeration.

Audit logging and monitoring are indispensable for detecting suspicious SMB activity. Windows Event Logs can capture detailed information about SMB access attempts, file modifications, deletions, and failed logins. Configuring audit policies to track both successful and failed access to sensitive SMB shares allows organizations to identify anomalies, such as an unusual volume of file changes or access attempts from unexpected devices. For greater visibility, logs should be forwarded to a centralized Security Information and Event Management (SIEM) platform, where automated alerts can notify security teams of potentially malicious activities.

Credential security is another cornerstone of SMB hardening. SMB authentication should leverage Kerberos wherever possible, as it provides mutual authentication and is more secure than NTLM. If NTLM is required for legacy systems, NTLMv2 should be enforced to minimize risk, and LM authentication should be completely disabled. Password policies should enforce strong password complexity, and organizations should implement multi-factor authentication (MFA) for administrative accounts to add an additional layer of protection against credential theft.

Administrative shares, such as ADMIN$, C$, and IPC$, should be tightly controlled. While these shares are created by default on Windows systems to facilitate remote management and administrative tasks, they also present a potential entry point for attackers who gain elevated privileges. Access to these shares should be restricted to designated administrative accounts, and unused administrative shares should be disabled to reduce the attack surface.

Implementing SMB client restrictions is equally important. Organizations can configure group policies to prevent clients from connecting to remote systems using SMB protocols that do not meet the organization's security baseline. Blocking outbound SMB connections to untrusted networks helps mitigate the risk of SMB relay attacks or data leakage caused by accidental connections to malicious servers.

Patch management is a fundamental aspect of hardening SMB. Many SMB vulnerabilities exploited in real-world attacks stem from unpatched systems. Regularly applying security updates to both

Windows and Linux systems running Samba ensures that known vulnerabilities are remediated and reduces the likelihood of exploitation. Automated patch management systems can help enforce timely updates, and critical patches should be prioritized in cases where vulnerabilities are being actively exploited in the wild.

In modern environments, organizations should also explore SMB over QUIC, a newer technology that encapsulates SMB traffic within the QUIC protocol. SMB over QUIC offers additional security benefits, such as leveraging TLS 1.3 for encryption, eliminating the need for traditional VPNs when accessing SMB shares from remote locations. This technology is particularly useful for organizations embracing hybrid work models where users require secure access to SMB shares without the overhead and complexity of VPN infrastructure.

Finally, user education is a critical yet often overlooked component of SMB hardening. Employees should be trained to recognize phishing attempts and social engineering tactics commonly used by attackers to gain initial access to systems. Awareness programs should emphasize the importance of reporting suspicious activity and following secure file-sharing practices, reducing the risk of internal users inadvertently exposing SMB services to exploitation.

By applying these hardening best practices, organizations can significantly reduce the risk of SMB being leveraged in cyberattacks. A multi-layered approach combining protocol hardening, network security, access control, monitoring, and user awareness forms the foundation of a secure SMB deployment. As threats targeting SMB continue to evolve, staying proactive with security controls and continuous improvement processes is essential to protect critical business data and maintain operational resilience.

# Intrusion Detection for SMB Traffic

Intrusion detection for SMB traffic is an essential component of a modern cybersecurity strategy aimed at identifying unauthorized or malicious activity within network environments. As SMB is widely used for file sharing, remote administration, and printer services across enterprise networks, it represents a critical service that is frequently targeted by cybercriminals. Detecting intrusions in SMB traffic enables organizations to recognize patterns of abuse, block ongoing attacks, and investigate incidents before they result in significant damage or data loss. SMB intrusion detection requires specialized tools and configurations, as SMB traffic often contains a mix of routine operations and potentially harmful behavior hidden in legitimate-looking requests.

SMB operates primarily over TCP port 445 and, in legacy configurations, over port 139 via NetBIOS. Its role in sharing resources across networks makes it a core service in most Windows environments, and its integration with Active Directory further deepens its presence in enterprise infrastructure. However, this broad deployment also creates a large attack surface. Threat actors often target SMB to gain unauthorized access, move laterally within networks, or deploy ransomware payloads. Therefore, placing SMB traffic under the scrutiny of intrusion detection systems is critical for identifying and mitigating threats in real-time.

Intrusion detection for SMB typically relies on network-based intrusion detection systems (NIDS) or intrusion prevention systems (IPS) that can inspect traffic at the packet level. Tools such as Snort, Suricata, and Zeek are among the most widely used open-source platforms capable of analyzing SMB traffic for suspicious behavior. These tools operate by capturing and analyzing packets as they traverse the network, comparing the data against a set of predefined rules or signatures that represent known attack patterns or anomalies. When a rule is matched, the IDS triggers an alert, notifying security teams of a potential intrusion.

Detecting SMB-based intrusions involves monitoring for several types of activity. Brute-force authentication attempts, where attackers repeatedly try different username and password combinations, are common. By observing a high volume of failed SMB login attempts from a single source or across multiple destinations, an intrusion detection system can flag the behavior as indicative of an account compromise attempt. SMB brute-force attacks are often precursors to ransomware deployments or data theft and must be detected early to prevent escalation.

Another critical aspect of SMB intrusion detection is identifying unauthorized enumeration attempts. Attackers frequently use tools to query SMB shares for information such as user lists, group memberships, and share names. These reconnaissance activities can reveal valuable details about the network's structure and the privileges associated with user accounts, enabling attackers to refine their attack strategies. Intrusion detection systems monitor SMB traffic for signs of enumeration techniques, such as repeated NetShareEnum, NetUserEnum, or NetGroupEnum requests, which could signal that an attacker is probing the network.

Suspicious file access patterns are also a telltale sign of malicious activity. Ransomware, for example, may generate large volumes of file access requests in rapid succession as it encrypts files within SMB shares. Similarly, mass deletions, renaming operations, or modifications to backup files may indicate a destructive attack in progress. By correlating the frequency and volume of SMB file operations with normal usage baselines, intrusion detection systems can highlight deviations that suggest active compromise or malware activity.

Intrusion detection for SMB also involves monitoring for known exploits targeting protocol vulnerabilities. This includes detecting exploit attempts against legacy SMB versions, such as SMBv1, which was notoriously vulnerable to the EternalBlue exploit. IDS platforms use signatures based on exploit payloads and traffic anomalies to identify these attacks. For instance, unusual SMB request structures, malformed headers, or atypical response sizes may trigger alerts for exploit attempts. As attackers continually refine their techniques, IDS rule sets are regularly updated by the security community to include new patterns reflecting the latest threat intelligence.

In environments where encrypted SMB sessions are used, such as with SMB 3.x encryption, intrusion detection becomes more challenging due to the inability to inspect the payload contents directly. However, even in encrypted scenarios, metadata such as connection frequency, file operation counts, and behavioral anomalies can still be analyzed. For example, detecting a sudden spike in encrypted SMB sessions originating from an unusual workstation could indicate malicious behavior, even if the payload itself remains unreadable to the IDS.

Integrating SMB intrusion detection with broader security tools enhances the overall defense strategy. For example, correlating SMB alerts with endpoint detection and response (EDR) telemetry can provide greater context around an incident. If an IDS detects a large number of SMB file encryption attempts, and the EDR simultaneously reports ransomware-like behavior on the same endpoint, security teams can validate the attack faster and initiate containment procedures. Integrating SMB intrusion alerts with a Security Information and Event Management (SIEM) system centralizes log collection and enables advanced analytics and correlation with other network events, such as failed VPN logins or lateral movement via Remote Desktop Protocol (RDP).

Advanced organizations may also implement custom IDS signatures tailored to their specific SMB environment. By analyzing normal SMB usage patterns within their network, security teams can write detection rules designed to flag activity outside of established baselines. This approach is particularly effective in high-security environments, where even minor deviations in SMB traffic could indicate an insider threat or a sophisticated attack attempting to blend in with legitimate operations.

Incident response workflows must be tightly coupled with SMB intrusion detection processes. When a potential SMB intrusion is detected, security teams should follow predefined escalation and investigation procedures. These may include isolating the affected endpoint, capturing additional packet data for forensic analysis, and reviewing file system logs on impacted servers to determine the scope of the incident. Time is often critical, especially in ransomware cases where early detection through SMB traffic analysis can prevent widespread encryption of shared files and mitigate damage.

Ultimately, intrusion detection for SMB traffic is not solely about blocking malicious activity but also about increasing visibility and awareness of how critical file-sharing infrastructure is being used. Without proper monitoring, SMB can serve as a silent vector for attackers to exfiltrate data, distribute malware, or gain unauthorized control over resources. By deploying intrusion detection mechanisms specifically tailored to analyze SMB communications, organizations can proactively detect and disrupt attacks targeting one of the most vital protocols in enterprise IT environments. This capability, when combined with other security controls such as SMB hardening, patch management, and network segmentation, helps organizations build a resilient and responsive cybersecurity posture.

# Implementing SMB Over QUIC

Implementing SMB over QUIC represents a modern evolution in securing and optimizing file-sharing capabilities, particularly in environments where traditional VPNs are not ideal. Server Message Block (SMB) has long been used to facilitate file sharing and network resource access across enterprise networks. However, with the rise of hybrid work, cloud services, and remote operations, there has been a growing demand for a more agile and secure way to access SMB shares across the internet. SMB over QUIC addresses this challenge by encapsulating SMB traffic within the QUIC protocol, providing an encrypted, reliable, and low-latency transport that is better suited for remote users and cloud-centric infrastructures.

QUIC, which stands for Quick UDP Internet Connections, is a transport layer protocol originally developed by Google and later standardized by the IETF. Unlike traditional TCP-based protocols, QUIC is designed to operate over UDP, offering features such as multiplexed connections, built-in encryption with TLS 1.3, and improved performance in networks with high latency or packet loss. Microsoft has integrated QUIC with SMB to allow organizations to provide secure file sharing without exposing TCP port 445, which is commonly blocked by firewalls and often associated with legacy vulnerabilities.

The implementation of SMB over QUIC begins by deploying the service on supported Windows platforms, such as Windows Server 2022 and Windows 11 Enterprise or Education editions. The server must be configured to listen for incoming QUIC connections over UDP port 443, which is typically used for HTTPS traffic and is widely allowed through firewalls and proxies. This change allows remote users to connect to corporate file shares without requiring a VPN, while maintaining the high security and encryption standards expected in modern enterprise environments.

To set up SMB over QUIC, administrators must first install the required Windows features, including the SMB over QUIC Server feature and the necessary IIS components that manage the QUIC listener. Once installed, the next step is to configure certificates to secure the QUIC connection using TLS 1.3. A valid X.509 certificate issued by a trusted certificate authority is required for the server, ensuring that clients can validate the server's identity during the handshake process. This certificate-based authentication provides strong protection against man-in-the-middle attacks and untrusted endpoints.

Configuration settings are managed through PowerShell or via Windows Admin Center, which simplifies the deployment process for administrators. Policies can define which SMB shares are made available over QUIC, which users or groups have access to them, and whether fallback to traditional SMB over TCP is permitted in case QUIC is unavailable. In most implementations, administrators prefer to prioritize QUIC for remote access while continuing to use SMB over TCP for internal, on-premises traffic.

SMB over QUIC offers significant advantages for remote and hybrid workforces. By leveraging UDP and QUIC's congestion control mechanisms, users experience reduced latency and improved performance when compared to SMB sessions over VPN tunnels, especially when operating in networks with unreliable connections, such as public Wi-Fi or cellular networks. Additionally, because SMB over QUIC tunnels traffic through UDP port 443, it can easily bypass restrictive network environments where traditional SMB ports or VPN protocols may be blocked.

Another key benefit of implementing SMB over QUIC is the elimination of VPN dependency for secure file sharing. VPNs, while widely used, introduce complexities such as client software installation, credential management, and performance overhead due to packet encapsulation. SMB over QUIC removes the need for these layers while still providing strong encryption and user authentication. This simplifies the remote access experience for employees and reduces administrative overhead for IT teams.

Security is a major focus in the design of SMB over QUIC. The use of TLS 1.3 ensures that all SMB traffic is encrypted in transit, including both file contents and metadata. Furthermore, SMB authentication via Kerberos or NTLM is fully supported, preserving the enterprise-grade identity and access control mechanisms of traditional SMB implementations. Additionally, QUIC's modern handshake process reduces the likelihood of downgrade attacks and minimizes the attack surface compared to older protocols.

For organizations adopting zero trust security models, SMB over QUIC aligns well with principles that prioritize secure-by-design connectivity and minimize implicit trust. By limiting SMB over QUIC access to specific users, groups, or device types, organizations can ensure that remote access to file shares is tightly controlled. Conditional access policies, combined with multifactor authentication, further enhance security by verifying both user identity and device posture before granting access to SMB shares.

Monitoring and managing SMB over QUIC is supported through event logging and performance counters available in Windows Server. Administrators can track metrics such as active QUIC sessions, data throughput, and handshake success rates. Integration with SIEM platforms allows security teams to correlate QUIC activity with broader network and endpoint events, helping to detect anomalies such as brute-force login attempts or unusual file access patterns. The visibility provided by these logs is critical for maintaining oversight of remote file-sharing activities and for incident response.

From an operational standpoint, SMB over QUIC simplifies connectivity for remote users who often struggle with VPN instability or geographic limitations imposed by restrictive network firewalls. By leveraging standard HTTPS port ranges and eliminating the need for additional tunneling, SMB over QUIC provides a seamless user experience, allowing employees to access corporate resources from anywhere without sacrificing security or performance.

However, successful deployment of SMB over QUIC also requires consideration of potential challenges. Administrators must ensure that DNS resolution for the SMB over QUIC endpoint is properly configured, often through split-brain DNS where internal and external queries resolve to different IP addresses based on the requester's location. This guarantees that internal users continue using SMB over TCP while remote users are directed to the SMB over QUIC listener. Additionally, organizations should regularly update Windows Server and client devices to ensure compatibility with the latest QUIC protocol enhancements and security patches.

Implementing SMB over QUIC represents a significant step forward in securing and optimizing remote access to SMB shares. Its design addresses many of the pain points associated with traditional VPNs while maintaining compatibility with existing Active Directory and file server infrastructures. For enterprises embracing cloud-first strategies and remote work flexibility, SMB over QUIC provides a scalable and secure file-sharing solution that aligns with modern security and networking best practices. As adoption of QUIC continues to grow across various services, integrating SMB into this protocol landscape positions organizations to deliver faster, safer, and more resilient connectivity for distributed workforces.

# SMB Multichannel and Network Resilience

SMB Multichannel is a feature introduced with SMB 3.0 that enhances the performance and resilience of SMB file transfers by enabling the use of multiple network connections simultaneously between an SMB client and server. In today's enterprise environments, where large file transfers, high availability, and system redundancy are critical, SMB Multichannel plays a vital role in maximizing the efficiency and fault tolerance of file sharing over the network. By intelligently distributing SMB traffic across multiple physical or virtual network interfaces, SMB Multichannel ensures that bandwidth is fully utilized and that communication between endpoints continues seamlessly even in the event of a network path failure.

At its core, SMB Multichannel detects available network interfaces on both the client and server, establishing multiple TCP connections between them. These connections operate in parallel, balancing the load of SMB sessions across each link to achieve higher throughput. This dynamic capability enables a client with multiple network adapters to aggregate bandwidth and take advantage of the combined speeds offered by each interface. For example, if both client and server have two gigabit Ethernet adapters, SMB Multichannel can leverage both links simultaneously, effectively doubling the available bandwidth for file transfers.

Beyond performance improvements, SMB Multichannel significantly enhances network resilience. In traditional SMB configurations that rely on a single TCP connection over a single network adapter, a failure in the adapter or network switch can immediately disrupt file-sharing operations. With SMB Multichannel, if one network path fails, the protocol automatically reroutes SMB traffic through the remaining available connections without interrupting the session. This failover behavior is seamless to users and applications, providing continuous access to shared files even in degraded network conditions.

SMB Multichannel is especially valuable in environments where redundancy is critical, such as data centers, virtualized infrastructures, and high-performance computing clusters. In these settings, servers often have multiple network interfaces connected to separate switches or network segments, forming part of a larger high-availability architecture. SMB Multichannel integrates naturally into this design by distributing traffic across these redundant paths and reacting to network failures or congestion events by rebalancing traffic as needed.

Administrators do not need to perform complex configurations to enable SMB Multichannel, as the feature is enabled by default on Windows Server 2012 and later versions, as well as on modern Windows clients such as Windows 10 and Windows 11. SMB Multichannel automatically detects the presence of multiple compatible network adapters and initiates additional SMB sessions accordingly. However, administrators should ensure that network adapters support RSS (Receive Side Scaling) or RDMA (Remote Direct Memory Access) to take full advantage of SMB Multichannel's capabilities. RSS allows network traffic to be distributed across multiple CPU cores, improving processing efficiency for large volumes of SMB traffic, while RDMA provides additional benefits by offloading network processing from the CPU to the network hardware.

In enterprise deployments, SMB Multichannel works in tandem with other advanced SMB features to optimize file-sharing performance. When combined with SMB Direct, which leverages RDMA-capable network cards, SMB Multichannel enables extremely high-speed, low-latency data transfers while reducing CPU utilization. This combination is particularly advantageous in scenarios such as Hyper-V live migrations, where virtual machines need to be moved between hosts without service interruption, or in Storage Spaces Direct deployments, where clustered storage nodes rely on efficient SMB communication to maintain data synchronization.

SMB Multichannel also improves user experience in branch office scenarios, where users may access file shares located at a central data center or regional hub. If WAN optimization appliances or SD-WAN solutions are in place, SMB Multichannel can balance traffic across both high-speed MPLS circuits and secondary internet-based VPN connections. In doing so, it helps maintain consistent file access speeds and reduces the impact of intermittent connectivity issues that might otherwise disrupt workflows.

Security is a key consideration when deploying SMB Multichannel. While it enhances performance and resilience, it is important to ensure that all network paths used by Multichannel are protected by appropriate security controls. SMB Multichannel supports all existing SMB security features, including SMB signing and encryption, ensuring that traffic spread across multiple links retains its integrity and confidentiality. Administrators should also review firewall configurations to ensure that all required TCP ports, such as port 445, are open across the intended network segments, while restricting access from untrusted or external networks.

Another consideration is the careful design of network topologies to fully benefit from SMB Multichannel. Ensuring that servers and clients have access to physically diverse network paths provides maximum fault tolerance. For instance, connecting network adapters to different switches or VLANs can protect against single points of failure in the network. Network interface teaming or bonding can also be used in conjunction with SMB Multichannel, but it is important to recognize that SMB Multichannel provides redundancy and load balancing at the

SMB protocol level, while NIC teaming operates at the network driver level.

Monitoring and troubleshooting SMB Multichannel is facilitated through built-in Windows tools. PowerShell commands such as Get-SmbMultichannelConnection and Get-SmbMultichannelSession allow administrators to view active multichannel connections, assess bandwidth usage per connection, and identify any connectivity issues affecting individual network paths. Event logs also capture multichannel-related events, providing visibility into when channels are added, removed, or failover events occur.

Organizations adopting hybrid cloud strategies can also leverage SMB Multichannel when accessing cloud-hosted file shares, such as those provided by Azure Files Premium tier. In such scenarios, virtual machines with multiple virtual NICs connected to Azure virtual networks can benefit from SMB Multichannel's load balancing and redundancy features, ensuring resilient access to cloud-based file shares.

Overall, SMB Multichannel represents a critical enhancement for enterprises seeking to optimize the performance, scalability, and reliability of their file-sharing infrastructure. As networks continue to evolve and organizations place a greater emphasis on hybrid work models, high availability, and business continuity, SMB Multichannel serves as a vital tool in delivering uninterrupted and efficient access to network resources. By combining multiple network paths into a unified, intelligent transport mechanism, it helps ensure that SMB services remain available, performant, and resilient in the face of growing demands and network complexities.

# Troubleshooting SMB Performance Issues

Troubleshooting SMB performance issues is a critical task for network administrators and IT professionals who manage enterprise file sharing environments. Slow or unreliable SMB file transfers can negatively impact productivity, hinder business operations, and create frustration for end users. Because SMB relies on a combination of network infrastructure, server configurations, client settings, and storage performance, identifying and resolving bottlenecks requires a comprehensive and methodical approach. Performance issues can arise from factors such as network latency, suboptimal protocol settings, resource contention on servers, client misconfigurations, or even security controls interfering with SMB traffic flow.

The first step in troubleshooting SMB performance problems is to isolate the scope and pattern of the issue. Administrators should determine whether the problem is widespread across the organization or isolated to specific users, servers, or geographic locations. If users in one office or connected to a particular file server are experiencing slow file access while others are unaffected, the issue may be localized to a specific network segment, server hardware, or configuration. Gathering details such as the time of day when slowness occurs, the size of files being transferred, and whether the performance issue affects all SMB shares or only specific ones provides valuable context.

Network latency and packet loss are among the most common causes of degraded SMB performance. SMB, particularly in versions prior to SMB 3.x, is sensitive to high-latency connections. Wide area networks, VPN tunnels, and unstable Wi-Fi networks can introduce significant delays in the transmission of SMB packets, leading to sluggish file transfers and slow browsing of network shares. Administrators should start by measuring network latency using tools such as ping or traceroute to identify delays between clients and servers. Packet capture tools like Wireshark can also reveal retransmissions, out-of-order packets, or excessive TCP resets that might indicate unstable network links.

Suboptimal SMB version usage is another factor that can limit performance. Clients and servers operating on outdated protocols such as SMB 1.0 may experience slower transfers due to the protocol's chattiness and lack of modern enhancements like pipelining, multichannel support, or large MTU sizes. Ensuring that both clients and servers are configured to negotiate the highest available SMB version, such as SMB 3.0 or SMB 3.1.1, allows them to benefit from performance features like SMB Direct and SMB Multichannel. Administrators should verify protocol versions using PowerShell commands such as Get-SmbConnection or by reviewing packet captures to identify the SMB dialect in use.

Server-side performance issues can also contribute to slow SMB operations. Insufficient CPU resources, high memory usage, or disk I/O bottlenecks on the file server can throttle SMB traffic, especially under heavy load. Administrators should monitor server performance using tools like Windows Performance Monitor to track key metrics such as CPU utilization, disk latency, network throughput, and memory usage. If storage arrays or disks exhibit high latency, replacing aging hardware, upgrading to faster drives, or optimizing RAID configurations may be necessary to restore acceptable file transfer speeds.

Misconfigured or overloaded network interface cards on the server or client can create another bottleneck. A single underperforming NIC, or one that lacks features like RSS or RDMA, may not handle the demands of large file transfers efficiently. In environments where SMB Multichannel is supported, but only one active NIC is being used, administrators should check whether additional NICs are available and properly configured. Enabling RSS on both the server and client can improve parallel processing of network traffic across CPU cores, while RDMA-enabled adapters can dramatically boost performance when SMB Direct is in use.

Security software and network appliances may inadvertently slow down SMB performance. Endpoint protection platforms, host-based firewalls, and deep packet inspection tools may introduce latency by inspecting each SMB packet for potential threats. While security controls are essential, configuring them to exclude trusted SMB traffic from unnecessary inspection can reduce delays without compromising safety. Additionally, SMB signing, while crucial for data integrity, introduces additional overhead by forcing each packet to be cryptographically signed and verified. In low-risk internal networks, where SMB encryption is also enabled, administrators may choose to disable mandatory signing to improve performance, provided that this aligns with the organization's security policies.

Group Policy settings and registry configurations can also affect SMB performance. Certain policies may restrict the maximum number of concurrent SMB sessions or limit cache sizes, reducing the ability of clients to efficiently browse shares and retrieve files. Reviewing and tuning relevant SMB-related policies, such as those that control offline files, client-side caching, or SMB client redirector settings, can help improve responsiveness. For example, enabling directory caching or increasing the cache timeout on clients can reduce the frequency of server queries, improving performance when navigating large directories.

Client-related issues must also be addressed during troubleshooting. Outdated network drivers, misconfigured power-saving settings, or poorly performing wireless adapters can degrade SMB file transfers. Ensuring that clients have up-to-date drivers, particularly for NICs and wireless adapters, is a basic but essential step. Administrators should also disable power-saving features that cause NICs to reduce throughput or enter low-power states during SMB transfers.

For larger file transfers or workloads that require consistent performance, administrators should consider implementing Quality of Service (QoS) policies to prioritize SMB traffic over other types of network traffic. QoS configurations on network switches and routers can prevent SMB traffic from competing with less critical data flows, helping maintain steady file transfer rates during periods of network congestion.

Advanced troubleshooting may involve conducting end-to-end testing in controlled environments to replicate the issue. Setting up a test client and server on isolated segments can help determine whether the problem is systemic or isolated to production infrastructure. Testing file transfers using different client operating systems or hardware platforms may reveal whether performance issues are linked to specific devices or configurations.

Ultimately, resolving SMB performance issues requires a holistic approach that considers network, server, client, and protocol factors. By systematically isolating each layer and applying targeted optimizations, administrators can restore efficient file-sharing operations and enhance the user experience. Continuous monitoring and proactive maintenance of the network and file-sharing environment further ensure that SMB performance remains consistent and resilient in dynamic enterprise settings.

# Optimizing SMB for WAN Environments

Optimizing SMB for WAN environments is critical for organizations that rely on remote offices, distributed teams, or hybrid cloud infrastructures where users access SMB shares across geographically dispersed locations. While SMB is highly effective on local area networks due to its efficiency and reliability, wide area networks introduce challenges such as high latency, packet loss, and limited bandwidth that can significantly degrade SMB performance. To address these challenges, organizations must employ a combination of network optimizations, protocol tuning, and architectural strategies that improve the responsiveness and resilience of SMB traffic over WAN links.

One of the main obstacles SMB faces over WAN environments is latency. SMB was originally designed for use within LANs, where round-trip times are minimal. On WAN connections, however, latency can introduce delays in file browsing, transfers, and metadata queries. Each SMB request and response is subject to WAN-induced delays, which can accumulate rapidly during operations involving multiple file or directory lookups. For instance, navigating a directory structure with hundreds of files over a high-latency link may feel sluggish due to the sheer number of SMB operations required to list the contents. Reducing the dependency on round-trip responses is key to mitigating the effects of latency.

To improve SMB performance across WANs, one of the most effective solutions is enabling SMB 3.x and above, as newer versions of the protocol introduce performance features tailored for non-LAN scenarios. SMB 3.x supports features such as SMB Multichannel, which allows clients and servers to use multiple network paths simultaneously for a single SMB session. When paired with WAN connections that have redundant paths, SMB Multichannel can aggregate available bandwidth and provide failover capabilities that reduce the impact of link failures or congestion.

Additionally, enabling SMB Direct with RDMA-capable network interfaces can further optimize performance, especially for data center-to-data center WAN links or in hybrid cloud scenarios where RDMA is supported. SMB Direct allows SMB traffic to bypass portions of the server's CPU and memory, reducing latency and improving throughput. While RDMA is less common on remote office connections, its use in backend data replication or storage traffic across WAN links can yield significant gains.

Data compression, introduced in SMB 3.1.1, also enhances performance in WAN environments. By reducing the size of SMB payloads, compression minimizes the amount of data that must traverse bandwidth-constrained WAN links, accelerating file transfers and reducing the strain on the network. Administrators can enable SMB compression at the server or share level, making it particularly useful for scenarios where large files, such as virtual machine images or media assets, are frequently accessed across long distances.

Another key tactic is the use of branch cache or offline files for remote offices. BranchCache is a WAN optimization technology integrated with Windows that caches SMB file content locally at branch sites. When enabled, users in remote locations retrieve cached versions of frequently accessed files, reducing the need to repeatedly download data from central file servers over the WAN. BranchCache operates in distributed or hosted cache modes, depending on whether a dedicated caching server is deployed at the branch or whether clients share cached data peer-to-peer. Offline files can also be configured to allow users to continue working on files locally when the WAN link is unavailable, with automatic synchronization when connectivity is restored.

Deploying WAN acceleration appliances can provide further improvements to SMB traffic performance. WAN optimizers from vendors such as Riverbed or Cisco employ techniques like deduplication, TCP optimization, and application-layer caching to reduce WAN bandwidth consumption and enhance throughput for SMB traffic. These devices inspect and modify SMB communications in real-time, streamlining data transfers and reducing redundant transmissions, particularly for workloads that involve repetitive access to similar data sets across the WAN.

Tuning TCP parameters can also contribute to SMB performance optimization over wide area networks. Adjustments such as increasing the TCP window size allow larger amounts of data to be in transit before requiring acknowledgment, compensating for high-latency links. Modern operating systems generally have auto-tuning features enabled by default, but administrators may still need to verify these settings and fine-tune them for specific WAN scenarios. Ensuring that both client and server TCP stacks are configured to handle larger receive and send buffers can mitigate bottlenecks caused by limited flow control windows on long-distance connections.

Network architecture plays a critical role as well. Implementing site-to-site VPN tunnels or leveraging SD-WAN solutions helps optimize SMB traffic routing across WANs. SD-WAN platforms dynamically select the most efficient path based on current network conditions, steering SMB traffic through lower-latency or higher-bandwidth connections as needed. SD-WAN also enables organizations to segment and prioritize SMB traffic using QoS policies, ensuring that file-sharing operations receive preferential treatment over non-critical network traffic.

File system design and share configuration further influence SMB performance over WAN links. Reducing the number of files and subfolders within directories can accelerate directory listing operations, while flattening deep directory structures can reduce the overhead associated with recursive SMB queries. Administrators should also avoid setting overly restrictive permissions that require excessive access control list (ACL) checks across large directory trees, as this can amplify latency in WAN environments.

Optimizing client settings is equally important. Enabling client-side caching mechanisms and tuning file explorer behavior, such as disabling automatic thumbnail generation when accessing remote shares, can reduce the number of metadata queries sent over the WAN. Adjustments like disabling Windows search indexing on SMB shares accessed over slow links can also improve responsiveness when navigating remote file shares.

Monitoring SMB traffic across WAN links is essential to validate the effectiveness of optimization efforts. Performance monitoring tools that capture SMB session metrics, such as latency, throughput, and error rates, help administrators identify bottlenecks and trends over time. Packet analysis tools like Wireshark can reveal low-level details of SMB conversations, exposing issues such as excessive retransmissions or inefficient protocol behavior under specific network conditions.

The combination of protocol enhancements, caching strategies, WAN optimization technologies, and thoughtful network design provides a solid foundation for improving SMB performance across WAN environments. By tailoring SMB implementations to the unique challenges of wide area networks, organizations can deliver faster, more reliable access to shared resources for remote offices, branch locations, and mobile users, ensuring that collaboration and business operations remain smooth and efficient, even across geographically distributed environments.

# SMB Load Balancing and Failover

SMB load balancing and failover are essential techniques in modern enterprise environments where high availability and efficient use of network resources are critical to ensuring business continuity and optimal performance. As organizations increasingly depend on centralized file servers and distributed storage systems to support their operations, the demand for robust SMB infrastructures capable of handling large volumes of concurrent connections and sustaining service during failures has grown significantly. Implementing load balancing and failover mechanisms for SMB helps distribute network traffic across multiple servers, improve resource utilization, reduce latency, and maintain uninterrupted file-sharing services in the event of hardware or network outages.

Load balancing in the context of SMB typically involves distributing SMB client requests across multiple file servers or network interfaces to prevent any single resource from becoming overwhelmed. This strategy is commonly deployed in environments with clustered file servers, such as Windows Failover Clusters or Storage Spaces Direct configurations, where multiple nodes work together to present SMB shares to clients. Load balancing ensures that client sessions are evenly spread among available servers or network paths, optimizing the use of compute, storage, and network resources.

One of the most widely used methods of implementing SMB load balancing is through the deployment of Scale-Out File Servers (SOFS) in Windows Server environments. A Scale-Out File Server allows multiple cluster nodes to simultaneously provide access to a single namespace or SMB share, with client connections automatically distributed across the nodes. This model enables high availability and balanced workloads without requiring complex manual configurations. When clients connect to the SMB share, the Cluster Name Object (CNO) used for the share resolves to multiple IP addresses through DNS round-robin or load-balancing-aware mechanisms such as SMB Multichannel.

SMB Multichannel itself is a native SMB protocol feature that enhances load balancing and failover by establishing multiple simultaneous TCP connections between a client and server across different network interfaces. By distributing SMB traffic across multiple NICs, SMB Multichannel provides automatic load balancing of SMB sessions at the protocol level and ensures redundancy in case one network path fails. This is particularly valuable in data centers where servers are equipped with multiple network interfaces connected to different switches, as it prevents a single point of failure from disrupting client access to file shares.

Network Load Balancing (NLB) is another common approach used to distribute SMB traffic across multiple servers. While NLB is more commonly associated with stateless services such as web servers, it can be applied to SMB environments where client connections are short-lived or when used in conjunction with distributed file systems. NLB directs client requests to different servers based on algorithms such as round-robin or least connections, helping to balance the load and prevent any single server from becoming a bottleneck. However, NLB may not be ideal for persistent SMB sessions or file locking scenarios, which are better handled by solutions like SOFS that support shared storage access across nodes.

In addition to server-level load balancing, DNS plays a role in directing SMB traffic to available resources. DNS round-robin techniques can assign multiple IP addresses to the same SMB share hostname, allowing clients to resolve to different servers during connection establishment. While simple and widely supported, DNS round-robin does not account for server load or real-time availability, making it most effective when combined with other load-balancing techniques or monitored DNS services that remove unhealthy nodes from the DNS rotation.

Failover capabilities are critical to complement load balancing strategies, ensuring that SMB services remain accessible in the event of hardware failures, network outages, or software issues. Windows Server Failover Clustering (WSFC) provides built-in failover functionality for SMB services, allowing virtual network names and SMB shares to move between nodes within a cluster if a node becomes unavailable. This automatic failover process minimizes downtime and protects against data loss by leveraging shared storage solutions such as Cluster Shared Volumes (CSV) or Storage Spaces Direct.

When deploying SMB failover solutions, it is important to configure client systems for resilience. Modern Windows clients are designed to automatically reconnect to available nodes within a failover cluster or reconnect SMB sessions across multiple connections established by SMB Multichannel. This seamless reconnection process is transparent to users and helps maintain productivity even when underlying infrastructure components experience disruptions.

Storage layer considerations also play a role in SMB failover and load balancing. Distributed file systems such as DFS Namespaces abstract multiple SMB shares behind a unified namespace, allowing administrators to create fault-tolerant and geographically distributed file structures. DFS can be configured with referral ordering and site-awareness to direct clients to the nearest or most responsive file server, improving performance and enhancing resilience against WAN outages or site-specific failures.

SMB Direct, used in conjunction with RDMA-enabled network interfaces, complements load balancing and failover strategies by enabling low-latency and high-throughput data transfers while providing automatic failover at the network layer. If an RDMA-capable path becomes unavailable, SMB Direct automatically reroutes traffic to other available RDMA paths or falls back to standard TCP-based SMB Multichannel connections.

Proactive monitoring and testing are essential to ensure that load balancing and failover configurations are functioning as intended. Administrators should conduct regular failover tests by simulating node or network failures and verifying that clients can seamlessly reconnect to alternate resources. Performance monitoring tools, such as Windows Performance Monitor and cluster validation tests within Failover Cluster Manager, provide insights into cluster health, node utilization, and network traffic distribution, helping administrators identify imbalances or misconfigurations that could impact performance or resilience.

In hybrid cloud environments, load balancing and failover principles extend to cloud-hosted file services. Solutions such as Azure Files Premium tier offer SMB shares with integrated load balancing across Microsoft's global network, providing remote offices and cloud workloads with high-availability SMB services. Pairing these services with technologies like Azure File Sync allows organizations to cache frequently accessed data locally while leveraging cloud resilience for disaster recovery scenarios.

Ultimately, SMB load balancing and failover are key components of a robust and scalable file-sharing architecture. By ensuring that client traffic is intelligently distributed across multiple servers and that services can withstand hardware or network failures, organizations can maintain high performance and availability for SMB-based file sharing. This resilience is crucial in environments where uptime and operational continuity are non-negotiable, making load balancing and failover indispensable elements of any enterprise SMB deployment.

# Leveraging DFS with SMB

Leveraging Distributed File System (DFS) with SMB allows organizations to create a scalable, fault-tolerant, and easy-to-navigate file-sharing infrastructure. DFS is a Microsoft technology that integrates with the Server Message Block protocol to provide a virtualized namespace, simplify access to geographically dispersed file shares, and enhance redundancy and availability across the enterprise. By abstracting the physical location of SMB shares behind a unified DFS namespace, users and applications can connect to shared folders without needing to know the actual server or path hosting the resource. This flexibility is particularly valuable in large and distributed environments where maintaining a clear and manageable file-sharing structure is essential.

DFS consists of two primary components: DFS Namespaces and DFS Replication. DFS Namespaces enable the creation of a logical folder hierarchy under a single root, which can link to multiple SMB shares located on different servers, sites, or regions. For example, an organization can publish shared folders from servers in multiple branch offices under a single DFS namespace such as \company.local\files. Users accessing the namespace see a consistent folder structure regardless of where the underlying data resides. This abstraction reduces user confusion, streamlines resource access, and simplifies network drive mapping and group policy configurations.

When integrated with SMB, DFS Namespaces provide seamless redirection of client requests to appropriate SMB shares known as folder targets. Each folder target in a DFS namespace corresponds to an SMB share hosted on a particular server. DFS leverages SMB to handle the actual file access, ensuring that clients interact with SMB shares using familiar protocols and security models. This integration allows organizations to retain the benefits of NTFS permissions, SMB signing, encryption, and access controls while presenting users with a unified and simplified view of available resources.

One of the key benefits of using DFS with SMB is site-awareness and referral ordering. DFS is capable of detecting a client's Active Directory site and directing them to the closest or most appropriate SMB server based on their physical or logical network location. This reduces WAN traffic by prioritizing access to local file servers rather than routing users to remote data centers or branch offices unnecessarily. By optimizing data paths in this way, DFS improves performance and minimizes latency, especially for large file transfers or collaborative workflows that rely heavily on shared resources.

DFS also provides load balancing capabilities by offering multiple folder targets for the same namespace entry. When multiple SMB shares host the same content, DFS can distribute client connections across these targets, balancing the load and reducing the risk of server saturation. Administrators can configure referral ordering policies to determine how DFS prioritizes targets, including options such as random ordering, lowest-cost ordering based on site proximity, or manual prioritization. This flexibility enables organizations to tailor DFS behavior according to network topology and business requirements.

For organizations seeking high availability and fault tolerance, DFS Replication complements DFS Namespaces by synchronizing data between SMB shares hosted on different servers. DFS Replication is a multi-master replication engine that uses Remote Differential Compression (RDC) to replicate only the changed portions of files, reducing bandwidth usage and accelerating synchronization across WAN links. By replicating critical file shares across multiple servers, DFS ensures that users can continue to access important resources even if one server or site becomes unavailable due to hardware failure, network outages, or scheduled maintenance.

DFS Replication also supports conflict resolution and versioning mechanisms that prevent data corruption or loss when simultaneous edits occur at different replication partners. Administrators can configure replication schedules, bandwidth throttling, and staging folder sizes to fine-tune replication performance according to available network capacity and business priorities. Combined with SMB's inherent support for file locking and access control, DFS Replication maintains data consistency and security across all replicated file servers.

DFS with SMB is also instrumental in supporting disaster recovery strategies. By replicating data across geographically separate locations, organizations can protect against data loss resulting from localized disasters such as power outages, hardware failures, or natural events. In the event of a failure at the primary site, users can be redirected to alternative DFS targets in secondary or tertiary locations, restoring access to mission-critical resources with minimal disruption.

Security remains an important consideration when implementing DFS with SMB. Since DFS relies on SMB for file access, all SMB-related security controls apply to DFS targets, including NTFS permissions, SMB encryption, and SMB signing. Administrators must ensure that folder targets are properly secured, with access permissions assigned according to the principle of least privilege. Additionally, to protect DFS Replication traffic across untrusted networks, organizations can implement IPsec or SMB encryption to ensure that data in transit remains confidential and tamper-proof.

DFS also simplifies administrative tasks by centralizing namespace management. Instead of managing separate SMB shares on individual servers, administrators can update, add, or remove folder targets within the DFS Management Console or via PowerShell. This reduces the administrative overhead associated with reconfiguring client-side mappings when servers are decommissioned or restructured, as the DFS namespace path remains consistent for end users.

When combined with Active Directory and Group Policy, DFS integration with SMB allows for automated deployment of mapped network drives based on user roles, departments, or locations. This further enhances the user experience, ensuring that employees always have access to the correct shared folders without manual configuration. Users benefit from a simplified folder structure and consistent paths, while IT departments gain flexibility in managing and scaling the file-sharing environment.

DFS with SMB also supports business scenarios involving mergers and acquisitions, where integrating file servers from different organizations into a single namespace is crucial. By linking disparate SMB shares under a common DFS namespace, administrators can provide a unified file-sharing experience without requiring immediate consolidation of physical storage systems. This facilitates smoother transitions and faster alignment of IT resources with evolving business objectives.

For organizations embracing hybrid cloud models, DFS can be extended to cloud-based SMB services such as Azure Files. By combining on-premises DFS Namespaces with cloud-hosted shares, businesses can create hybrid environments where users access both local and cloud resources under a single namespace. This approach supports scenarios such as cloud-based disaster recovery, content offloading to cloud storage, and improved accessibility for remote and mobile users.

Ultimately, leveraging DFS with SMB enables organizations to build highly available, flexible, and user-friendly file-sharing infrastructures. By abstracting complexity, optimizing resource utilization, and improving network efficiency, DFS combined with SMB provides a scalable solution for meeting the demands of modern enterprise environments. As businesses continue to expand globally and adopt hybrid IT strategies, DFS remains a cornerstone technology for simplifying file access while enhancing performance, resilience, and administrative control.

# Storage Solutions Integrating SMB

Storage solutions that integrate with the Server Message Block protocol have become indispensable components of modern IT infrastructure, enabling organizations to provide centralized file-sharing capabilities to users and applications. SMB is a key protocol for accessing networked file storage, allowing seamless interaction with files, folders, and shared resources across LAN, WAN, and hybrid cloud environments. Whether deployed in traditional data centers or modern cloud-first architectures, storage solutions that support SMB provide the foundation for collaborative workflows, data centralization, and secure file access in both small and large enterprises.

Network Attached Storage, or NAS, systems are among the most common storage solutions that integrate SMB. NAS devices are purpose-built file servers that provide shared storage over the network using file-sharing protocols such as SMB, NFS, and AFP. In environments where Windows clients are prevalent, NAS systems configured with SMB offer a familiar and compatible interface for file sharing. Major NAS vendors like Synology, QNAP, and NetApp offer comprehensive SMB implementations that include support for advanced features such as SMB Multichannel, SMB Direct, and SMB encryption. These devices allow administrators to quickly provision shared folders, define access control through Active Directory integration, and enforce security policies, all while providing users with easy access to files via mapped drives or UNC paths.

Enterprise storage solutions also leverage SMB through integrated storage appliances and unified storage platforms. These solutions often combine block-level protocols such as iSCSI and Fibre Channel with file-level protocols like SMB and NFS, offering organizations flexibility in how they deploy storage depending on workload requirements. Unified storage arrays from vendors like Dell EMC, NetApp, and Hewlett Packard Enterprise provide SMB-based file shares as part of their core capabilities, enabling IT teams to serve both virtualized workloads and user file shares from a single, centralized storage system.

In addition to hardware appliances, software-defined storage (SDS) platforms have become a popular option for integrating SMB file services. SDS solutions abstract storage resources from physical hardware, creating virtualized pools of storage that can be provisioned and accessed via SMB shares. Microsoft's Storage Spaces Direct, for instance, allows Windows Server clusters to aggregate locally attached disks across multiple nodes and present highly available SMB shares. By utilizing SMB 3.x features such as SMB Direct and SMB Multichannel, Storage Spaces Direct enhances the performance and resiliency of SMB shares in hyper-converged infrastructures.

Cloud-based storage solutions have further expanded the reach of SMB. Microsoft Azure Files is a fully managed cloud file-sharing service that exposes SMB shares natively to Windows, Linux, and macOS clients. Azure Files supports SMB 3.x with encryption, enabling secure file access over the internet without requiring VPN connectivity. Organizations can integrate Azure Files with on-premises Active Directory for identity and access management, providing a hybrid model where users access both on-premises and cloud-based SMB shares under unified permissions and security policies. Azure File Sync complements this solution by enabling organizations to replicate and cache Azure file shares on local Windows Servers, optimizing performance for remote or branch offices.

In hybrid cloud deployments, many enterprises leverage cloud storage gateways to integrate on-premises SMB shares with cloud object storage platforms like Amazon S3 or Azure Blob Storage. These gateways act as intermediaries, presenting SMB shares to users while automatically tiering or archiving data to cloud storage backends based on policies such as file age or access frequency. This approach helps reduce costs by keeping infrequently accessed data in lower-cost cloud storage while maintaining fast, local access to active files.

Virtualization environments also depend heavily on storage solutions that integrate with SMB. Hyper-V, Microsoft's virtualization platform, can use SMB 3.x file shares as storage locations for virtual machine (VM) files, including VHDX disks and configuration data. This functionality allows VM workloads to reside on remote SMB shares while still supporting advanced Hyper-V features such as live migration and failover clustering. Leveraging SMB in this manner eliminates the need for traditional SAN storage, simplifying storage architectures and reducing infrastructure costs without sacrificing performance or availability.

Backup and disaster recovery solutions are another key use case for SMB-integrated storage. Many backup software platforms, including Veeam and Commvault, support writing backup files directly to SMB shares hosted on NAS devices, Windows Servers, or cloud-based SMB services like Azure Files. Using SMB for backup repositories allows organizations to centralize and secure backup data while streamlining recovery operations. Furthermore, combining SMB with features like DFS Replication or native snapshot capabilities on storage appliances enhances the resilience and recoverability of backup data.

Organizations that require high-performance computing (HPC) or big data processing may also leverage SMB-integrated storage solutions to support large-scale data access. In such environments, storage solutions with SMB Direct and RDMA-enabled network adapters deliver low-latency and high-throughput file access, enabling efficient data movement for analytics workloads, media rendering, or scientific simulations. Storage vendors often tailor SMB implementations for

HPC use cases by optimizing for parallel access patterns and reducing metadata overhead, ensuring that performance demands are met even in highly transactional environments.

Security remains a critical consideration when deploying SMB-integrated storage solutions. Organizations must implement strict access control policies using Active Directory groups and NTFS permissions to ensure that only authorized users can access sensitive data. SMB encryption and SMB signing should be enforced for traffic traversing untrusted networks to prevent eavesdropping and tampering. Storage appliances and cloud SMB services typically provide audit logging features, allowing administrators to monitor access patterns, detect anomalies, and maintain compliance with regulations such as GDPR, HIPAA, and PCI DSS.

In modern enterprise architectures, SMB-integrated storage solutions often form part of larger data management and collaboration ecosystems. File-sharing platforms like Microsoft SharePoint and Teams, for example, often rely on backend SMB file shares to store shared documents and media files. Integrating these platforms with scalable SMB storage solutions ensures that collaborative tools have the backend infrastructure needed to support growing data volumes and complex access patterns.

Overall, storage solutions integrating SMB play a pivotal role in enabling efficient, secure, and flexible file sharing within organizations. From traditional NAS devices to cloud-native services and hyper-converged infrastructure platforms, the ubiquity of SMB support across storage technologies ensures seamless interoperability with client devices and applications. As businesses continue to embrace digital transformation and distributed work models, the demand for scalable and resilient SMB-based storage solutions will only continue to grow, reinforcing SMB's position as a cornerstone of enterprise IT.

# Hybrid Cloud and SMB

Hybrid cloud and SMB represent a powerful combination for organizations aiming to modernize their IT infrastructure while maintaining control over critical data. As businesses increasingly embrace hybrid cloud strategies, blending on-premises systems with public cloud services, SMB continues to play a central role in bridging traditional file sharing with modern cloud-based workflows. SMB's versatility, compatibility with enterprise applications, and integration with cloud storage platforms make it a key enabler of hybrid environments, where data and applications are distributed across both private data centers and cloud services.

In a hybrid cloud model, organizations retain certain workloads and data sets within their own data centers while extending other services to public cloud platforms such as Microsoft Azure, Amazon Web Services, or Google Cloud. SMB facilitates seamless access to shared files across these disparate environments, ensuring users experience a unified and familiar interface for file storage regardless of where the underlying data resides. This integration reduces complexity for end users, who continue accessing SMB shares through standard UNC paths or mapped drives, while IT teams manage the backend using a combination of on-premises servers and cloud services.

A common approach to integrating SMB into hybrid cloud environments involves extending on-premises file shares to the cloud using services like Azure Files. Azure Files is a fully managed cloud file share service that supports the SMB 3.x protocol, allowing users and applications to access cloud-hosted file shares with the same tools and processes used in traditional data center environments. Azure Files supports SMB encryption for data in transit and integrates natively with Azure Active Directory Domain Services or on-premises Active Directory via Azure AD DS, enabling organizations to enforce consistent identity and access management policies across both cloud and on-premises SMB shares.

Hybrid cloud scenarios often leverage Azure File Sync to create an intelligent caching mechanism between cloud SMB shares and on-premises Windows Servers. With Azure File Sync, frequently accessed files are cached locally at branch offices or remote sites, reducing latency and bandwidth consumption for users who interact with SMB shares on a daily basis. Meanwhile, the full dataset resides in the cloud, where it benefits from cloud-scale durability, high availability, and simplified backup and recovery processes. This model enhances user productivity by combining the speed of local file access with the flexibility and scalability of cloud storage.

Another way hybrid cloud and SMB intersect is through disaster recovery and business continuity strategies. Organizations can replicate critical SMB shares to cloud storage platforms to create offsite copies of important data. In the event of a disaster, such as a data center outage or ransomware attack, users can be redirected to SMB shares hosted in the cloud, maintaining access to essential files while recovery efforts are underway. SMB's ability to operate across WAN and internet connections, particularly when combined with VPN or SMB over QUIC technologies, makes it well-suited for such hybrid continuity scenarios.

Hybrid cloud architectures also benefit from using SMB for centralized collaboration hubs that serve distributed teams. Files stored on-premises via SMB shares can be integrated with collaboration platforms like Microsoft Teams and SharePoint Online, enabling hybrid workforces to access, co-author, and share documents securely from virtually anywhere. Through cloud file services that expose SMB interfaces, teams across different locations and network boundaries can collaborate without the need to manually synchronize files or deploy complex middleware.

Security remains a critical focus when deploying SMB within hybrid cloud environments. Data moving between on-premises systems and cloud-hosted SMB shares must be protected from interception and tampering. SMB 3.x supports end-to-end encryption and session signing, safeguarding SMB traffic across hybrid links. Additionally, administrators can enforce strict access controls using NTFS permissions and integrate with multifactor authentication (MFA) systems to ensure that only authorized users can access sensitive hybrid cloud shares.

Network connectivity is a crucial factor in optimizing SMB performance in hybrid cloud deployments. Organizations may establish site-to-site VPNs, ExpressRoute connections, or SD-WAN overlays to create dedicated and secure links between on-premises networks and the cloud. These private or optimized network paths reduce latency and improve the reliability of SMB traffic, especially when dealing with large file transfers or latency-sensitive applications. SMB Multichannel and SMB Direct can further enhance performance across hybrid links by enabling bandwidth aggregation and leveraging RDMA-capable network interfaces where available.

Hybrid cloud and SMB also facilitate data lifecycle management and cost optimization strategies. By tiering infrequently accessed files from on-premises SMB shares to cloud-based object storage or archive tiers, organizations can reduce storage costs while maintaining accessibility through the SMB namespace. Many cloud providers offer storage lifecycle policies that automatically transition cold data to lower-cost storage classes while keeping it available for retrieval via SMB or other file-sharing protocols.

In hybrid cloud environments where compliance and data sovereignty are key concerns, SMB's integration with DFS Namespaces enables administrators to present a single, unified view of file shares while hosting data across multiple geographic locations. By deploying SMB shares in both local and cloud regions and configuring DFS referral ordering based on user location, organizations can meet regulatory requirements for data locality while delivering a consistent user experience across sites.

Containerized and microservices-based applications running in hybrid cloud environments may also interact with SMB shares to store and retrieve configuration files, logs, and shared datasets. Kubernetes clusters, for example, can mount SMB shares as persistent volumes for stateful workloads, enabling seamless data sharing between cloud-native applications and traditional file servers. This hybrid integration empowers organizations to modernize their application architectures without disrupting existing SMB-based workflows or access patterns.

Advanced hybrid cloud use cases may combine SMB with automation and orchestration tools such as Azure Automation, AWS Systems Manager, or PowerShell DSC. By automating the provisioning and management of SMB shares across on-premises and cloud environments, IT teams can streamline processes such as user onboarding, quota management, and access reviews, reducing administrative overhead and improving operational efficiency.

Ultimately, hybrid cloud and SMB work together to provide organizations with a flexible, scalable, and secure file-sharing framework that supports modern business needs. By extending SMB capabilities into the cloud while maintaining on-premises infrastructure, enterprises gain the ability to adapt to evolving operational demands, support remote workforces, and leverage cloud scalability, all while protecting critical assets and maintaining a unified data access experience for end users. As hybrid cloud adoption continues to grow, SMB will remain a critical component of enterprise architectures, enabling organizations to unlock new levels of agility and resilience in their IT operations.

# SMB in Microsoft Azure

SMB in Microsoft Azure provides organizations with a robust and scalable solution for file sharing that integrates seamlessly with cloud-native services and hybrid cloud deployments. As businesses transition to the cloud to modernize IT infrastructure and meet the demands of distributed workforces, Azure's support for SMB-based storage enables enterprises to extend traditional file-sharing protocols into the Microsoft cloud platform. Azure offers fully managed SMB file shares through the Azure Files service, empowering organizations to deliver secure and accessible file services without the need to manage on-premises storage hardware or complex configurations.

Azure Files supports the SMB 3.x protocol, which brings essential security and performance enhancements such as encryption in transit, SMB Multichannel, and durable handles for improved reliability. SMB in Azure is designed to provide compatibility with Windows, macOS, and Linux clients, allowing users to mount file shares and access them using familiar tools such as Windows Explorer, command-line utilities, or network drive mappings. This ensures a smooth transition for organizations shifting workloads to the cloud while maintaining continuity with existing file-sharing workflows.

One of the primary advantages of using SMB in Azure is the elimination of hardware management responsibilities traditionally associated with on-premises file servers or NAS devices. Azure Files is a fully managed Platform-as-a-Service (PaaS) offering, meaning Microsoft handles all aspects of infrastructure maintenance, including scaling, patching, and high availability. Organizations can quickly provision new SMB shares through the Azure portal, Azure CLI, or automated templates, making it easy to expand storage capacity and adapt to changing business requirements without capital expenditures on physical storage devices.

Azure Files integrates tightly with Azure Active Directory Domain Services (Azure AD DS), enabling administrators to apply NTFS permissions and manage file share access using existing Active Directory groups and user accounts. This integration allows organizations to enforce consistent identity and access management across hybrid environments, where users may access SMB shares hosted both on-premises and in Azure. Additionally, organizations can synchronize on-premises Active Directory with Azure AD DS to maintain a unified security model and simplify authentication processes for remote or cloud-based users.

The support for SMB encryption in Azure Files ensures that all data in transit is protected against eavesdropping and man-in-the-middle attacks, which is particularly important when SMB shares are accessed over public networks. SMB encryption is enabled by default for Azure Files, aligning with industry best practices and compliance requirements. Azure also provides comprehensive logging and monitoring tools through Azure Monitor and Azure Storage Analytics, allowing administrators to track access patterns, audit file share activity, and detect potential anomalies in real time.

In addition to standard file-sharing scenarios, SMB in Microsoft Azure supports more advanced use cases such as hosting profile containers for remote desktop environments, application data storage for cloud-hosted services, and hybrid storage models where Azure Files is used in conjunction with on-premises Windows Servers. Azure File Sync extends SMB capabilities by enabling administrators to replicate cloud-hosted SMB shares to multiple Windows Servers located in branch offices or remote sites. This hybrid model ensures that frequently accessed files are cached locally, providing fast access to data while minimizing the need for constant WAN traffic.

For development and testing purposes, Azure Files offers a convenient and flexible storage backend that can be accessed programmatically via the REST API or standard SMB mounts. Developers building applications on Azure can leverage SMB shares for temporary file storage, shared resources, or log aggregation, streamlining the integration of file storage into cloud-native solutions.

Another key benefit of SMB in Azure is its ability to support lift-and-shift migrations for legacy applications that rely on SMB for data storage. Many traditional business applications are tightly coupled to SMB shares for file storage, configuration data, or shared resources. By migrating these SMB shares to Azure Files, organizations can move their legacy applications to Azure-hosted virtual machines without rearchitecting storage layers, accelerating cloud adoption while reducing disruption to critical business systems.

Azure Files Premium, a high-performance tier of the Azure Files service, provides enhanced performance for workloads requiring low-latency and high-throughput SMB access. Premium shares are backed by solid-state drives (SSDs) and are optimized for IO-intensive workloads such as databases, media processing pipelines, and analytics applications. This tier also supports large file sizes and high file count scenarios, making it suitable for enterprises with demanding data storage requirements.

Additionally, Azure Files Standard tier, which leverages hard disk-based storage, offers a cost-effective option for less demanding workloads or archival purposes. Organizations can combine both Premium and Standard tiers to align storage costs with performance requirements, creating a balanced approach that maximizes resource efficiency across different use cases.

Azure also enables organizations to configure private endpoints for SMB shares, which allow secure access to Azure Files over Microsoft's private network backbone instead of the public internet. By using private endpoints, enterprises can further reduce exposure to external threats while maintaining optimal performance and consistent access controls. Private endpoints are a crucial component of a defense-in-depth strategy when deploying SMB shares within sensitive environments that handle regulated or confidential data.

For multi-region enterprises, Azure Files Geo-redundant Storage (GRS) and Zone-redundant Storage (ZRS) options provide enhanced resilience and availability by replicating data across multiple Azure regions or availability zones. This ensures that SMB shares remain accessible even during regional outages or datacenter failures, aligning with business continuity and disaster recovery objectives.

To support automation and infrastructure-as-code practices, Azure Files allows administrators to provision and manage SMB shares programmatically using Azure Resource Manager (ARM) templates, Terraform, or PowerShell scripts. This capability simplifies large-scale deployments and streamlines the integration of SMB file shares into CI/CD pipelines, making it easier for DevOps teams to manage cloud resources consistently across different environments.

SMB in Microsoft Azure complements broader Azure ecosystem services, including Azure Backup and Azure Security Center. Administrators can leverage Azure Backup to create regular snapshots of SMB shares, protecting critical data from accidental deletion, corruption, or ransomware attacks. Azure Security Center provides advanced threat protection by continuously assessing SMB shares for vulnerabilities, misconfigurations, or unauthorized access attempts, helping organizations maintain a strong security posture in the cloud.

By combining SMB's ubiquitous file-sharing capabilities with Azure's global infrastructure, organizations can deliver scalable, secure, and highly available storage solutions that support a wide range of workloads. Whether used to replace aging on-premises file servers, extend storage capacity to the cloud, or support hybrid and cloud-native applications, SMB in Microsoft Azure remains a critical component of enterprise storage strategies in today's digital landscape.

# SMB and Amazon FSx

SMB and Amazon FSx represent a powerful combination for organizations that require scalable, secure, and fully managed file storage solutions within the Amazon Web Services (AWS) cloud ecosystem. Amazon FSx provides a family of managed file systems designed to integrate seamlessly with Windows environments and enterprise applications that rely on the SMB protocol for file access and sharing. By supporting SMB natively, Amazon FSx allows businesses to migrate or extend their existing on-premises file services to the cloud without rearchitecting applications or changing established workflows.

Amazon FSx for Windows File Server is purpose-built to deliver fully managed Windows file systems that support the SMB protocol. It offers compatibility with SMB 2.0 through SMB 3.1.1, providing essential security features such as SMB encryption, SMB signing, and support for Windows Access Control Lists (ACLs). This means that administrators can enforce fine-grained permissions on files and folders using familiar NTFS security models, maintaining consistency with on-premises Active Directory-based environments. FSx integrates directly with AWS Managed Microsoft AD or self-managed Active Directory deployments, enabling single sign-on capabilities and centralized authentication for users accessing SMB shares hosted in AWS.

One of the core benefits of using SMB with Amazon FSx is the elimination of the operational overhead traditionally associated with managing file servers. AWS automates server maintenance, patching, backups, and high-availability configurations, allowing IT teams to focus on strategic initiatives rather than infrastructure management. FSx for Windows File Server offers multi-Availability Zone (multi-AZ) deployments that provide automatic failover and high availability within AWS regions. This ensures that SMB shares remain accessible even if an Availability Zone experiences an outage.

Performance is another area where Amazon FSx excels when delivering SMB file shares. FSx is backed by SSD storage, offering low-latency and high-throughput file access for workloads that require rapid data retrieval, such as content management systems, development environments, and database workloads storing files on network-attached SMB shares. FSx also allows administrators to select performance and throughput levels based on workload requirements. The storage capacity and throughput can be independently scaled, giving organizations the flexibility to match file system performance with changing business needs.

Amazon FSx supports Distributed File System (DFS) Namespaces, which enables organizations to unify multiple SMB shares under a single logical namespace, providing users with a consistent view of file shares across hybrid environments. By combining DFS with SMB on FSx, businesses can simplify file access for users while distributing the backend storage across AWS and on-premises locations. This integration is particularly useful for global enterprises seeking to standardize file access across different regions and reduce user complexity when navigating large directory structures.

Amazon FSx plays a significant role in hybrid cloud scenarios. Organizations often extend their on-premises Active Directory to AWS using AWS Directory Service or deploy AWS Direct Connect and VPN connections to securely link their data centers to the cloud. SMB shares hosted on FSx can then be accessed seamlessly by on-premises users and workloads running on Amazon EC2 instances or remote desktops within Amazon WorkSpaces. This hybrid model allows businesses to offload storage to FSx while maintaining local authentication and preserving user experience consistency across environments.

For backup and disaster recovery strategies, FSx provides automatic daily backups of SMB file systems, which are stored in Amazon S3. Administrators can also initiate manual backups or integrate FSx with AWS Backup for more granular backup scheduling and retention policies. These capabilities ensure that SMB file shares are protected against data loss due to accidental deletions, hardware failures, or ransomware attacks. Additionally, Amazon FSx supports point-in-time restore functionality, allowing organizations to quickly recover file systems to a previous state.

Amazon FSx's integration with AWS Identity and Access Management (IAM) also enhances security by controlling administrative access to FSx resources. While SMB file access is managed through Active Directory and NTFS permissions, IAM policies govern who can create, delete, or modify FSx file systems at the AWS infrastructure level. This layered security approach ensures that only authorized personnel can perform sensitive administrative operations within the AWS environment.

Administrators can monitor FSx SMB file system performance and health using Amazon CloudWatch metrics and alarms. Key metrics such as throughput, IOPS, disk usage, and file system status provide valuable insights into resource utilization and help teams proactively identify and address performance bottlenecks or capacity issues. Logs from SMB sessions and authentication attempts can also be integrated with AWS CloudTrail, providing comprehensive audit trails for security and compliance reporting.

Beyond traditional Windows workloads, FSx SMB shares can be accessed by Linux-based systems that support SMB clients, enabling cross-platform file sharing in mixed-OS environments. This flexibility is valuable in organizations where both Windows and Linux systems need to collaborate on shared file repositories, such as media production studios, research labs, or software development teams working on cross-platform projects.

Amazon FSx for Windows File Server also supports the use of SMB with Amazon AppStream 2.0 and Amazon WorkSpaces, providing scalable cloud desktops and application streaming solutions. By mounting FSx SMB shares to virtual desktop instances, businesses can deliver seamless access to user profiles, shared drives, and application data for remote employees or contractors. This centralized approach improves data governance while supporting secure remote work scenarios.

For enterprises migrating to the cloud, FSx simplifies the process of lifting and shifting legacy applications that depend on SMB storage. Many enterprise resource planning (ERP) systems, line-of-business (LOB) applications, and legacy file-serving solutions require direct integration with SMB shares for data storage or configuration management. By migrating these SMB shares to FSx, organizations can modernize infrastructure while preserving application functionality, accelerating cloud adoption without the need for major application refactoring.

Amazon FSx and SMB together provide a scalable, secure, and flexible file storage platform that supports a wide range of enterprise use cases. From hybrid deployments and disaster recovery to high-performance workloads and remote work solutions, FSx enhances the value of SMB by offering managed file services deeply integrated with the AWS ecosystem. By leveraging FSx for SMB-based storage needs, organizations can improve operational efficiency, strengthen security, and unlock new possibilities for innovation within the cloud.

# Network Security Fundamentals

Network security fundamentals are the core principles and practices designed to protect the integrity, confidentiality, and availability of data as it is transmitted and processed across interconnected systems. In today's digital landscape, organizations rely heavily on complex networks to share information, support operations, and provide access to applications and resources. However, this interconnectivity introduces risks, as cyber threats continuously evolve in sophistication and frequency. Understanding the foundational concepts of network security is critical to safeguarding both enterprise environments and personal data from unauthorized access, data breaches, and service disruptions.

At its most basic level, network security aims to control who has access to a network, what resources they can use, and how they interact with sensitive data. It also involves implementing controls that detect, prevent, and respond to potential security incidents. The concept of perimeter security was historically the first line of defense, where organizations established clear boundaries between trusted internal networks and untrusted external networks, such as the internet. Firewalls were deployed at these boundaries to filter traffic based on pre-defined rules, allowing or denying packets based on criteria such as IP addresses, protocols, and port numbers. While firewalls remain essential, modern network architectures require more granular and dynamic defenses as threats increasingly originate from both outside and inside the network.

Authentication and access control are critical pillars of network security. Authentication verifies the identity of users and devices attempting to access network resources, typically through credentials such as usernames, passwords, and multifactor authentication methods. Once authenticated, access control mechanisms enforce policies that limit what users and devices can do within the network. This includes restricting access to specific servers, applications, or data sets based on the principle of least privilege, which states that users should have only the minimum level of access required to perform their tasks. Directory services such as Microsoft Active Directory play a key role in implementing centralized authentication and access control across enterprise environments.

Network segmentation is another fundamental strategy for reducing the attack surface and containing security incidents. By dividing the network into distinct zones or segments, organizations can limit lateral movement by attackers who have compromised one part of the network. Segmentation can be physical, using separate switches and routers, or logical, using virtual LANs (VLANs) and software-defined networking (SDN) technologies. Critical assets, such as servers storing sensitive customer data or intellectual property, are typically isolated from less secure zones like guest Wi-Fi networks or public-facing web servers. Implementing segmentation ensures that breaches in one zone do not easily propagate to the entire network.

Encryption is a cornerstone of protecting data in transit across networks. Transport Layer Security (TLS) and IPsec are two widely used protocols that provide end-to-end encryption of data exchanged between endpoints, shielding it from eavesdropping and tampering by unauthorized parties. TLS is commonly used to secure web traffic and application communication, while IPsec can encrypt entire network tunnels between sites or remote users and corporate networks. In addition to encrypting traffic, many organizations enforce encryption at rest to protect data stored on servers and storage devices, further enhancing overall security.

Intrusion detection and prevention systems (IDPS) are essential tools for monitoring network traffic and identifying potential threats. An intrusion detection system (IDS) analyzes packets for signatures of known attacks or behavioral anomalies that suggest malicious activity.

An intrusion prevention system (IPS) takes this a step further by actively blocking traffic that matches suspicious patterns. These systems provide visibility into real-time threats, including malware infections, brute-force login attempts, and exploitation of known vulnerabilities, allowing security teams to respond promptly to incidents.

Network security also relies heavily on endpoint protection. While network-level defenses are vital, the devices that connect to the network—such as laptops, servers, and IoT devices—must be secured against compromise. Antivirus software, host-based firewalls, and endpoint detection and response (EDR) solutions help detect and contain threats on individual devices, preventing them from becoming footholds for attackers. EDR tools, in particular, provide advanced threat detection by analyzing endpoint behaviors and enabling rapid investigation and remediation of incidents.

Security information and event management (SIEM) systems are integral to a well-rounded network security strategy. SIEM platforms aggregate logs and event data from network devices, servers, applications, and security tools, correlating events to detect suspicious activity and generate actionable alerts. By providing centralized visibility into network activity, SIEM solutions help security teams identify patterns of compromise, investigate incidents, and comply with regulatory requirements through detailed audit trails and reporting.

Modern network security also involves securing wireless networks, which are inherently more susceptible to unauthorized access due to the open nature of radio frequency communications. Best practices include implementing strong Wi-Fi encryption standards such as WPA3, enforcing complex passphrase policies, and using network access control (NAC) systems to ensure that only compliant and authorized devices can connect to wireless networks. Guest wireless access should always be segmented from internal networks to prevent untrusted users from reaching critical systems.

The human element is another critical component of network security. Social engineering attacks, such as phishing, rely on manipulating users to disclose sensitive information or execute malicious actions.

Regular security awareness training educates employees on identifying and responding to such threats, fostering a security-conscious culture within the organization. Additionally, clearly defined incident response plans ensure that when breaches occur, teams are prepared to contain and remediate threats efficiently.

Network security fundamentals continue to evolve in response to new challenges presented by trends such as cloud computing, remote work, and bring-your-own-device (BYOD) policies. In cloud environments, traditional perimeter defenses may be insufficient, leading to the adoption of zero trust architectures. Zero trust assumes that no device or user, even those inside the corporate network, should be trusted by default. Instead, continuous authentication, strict access controls, and real-time monitoring are enforced to minimize risk. Implementing zero trust principles enhances network security by reducing reliance on static perimeters and focusing on dynamic, identity-based access management.

Ultimately, network security fundamentals lay the groundwork for building a secure IT environment that protects organizational assets, ensures regulatory compliance, and supports business continuity. As cyber threats grow more sophisticated, organizations must remain vigilant, continuously updating their defenses and adapting to emerging risks to safeguard their networks and the sensitive data they carry.

# Threat Modeling for SMB Networks

Threat modeling for SMB networks is an essential process aimed at identifying, understanding, and mitigating potential security threats that could compromise the confidentiality, integrity, or availability of resources shared through the Server Message Block protocol. SMB networks are a common component in enterprise environments, providing file sharing, printer access, and remote management capabilities across Windows and mixed-OS infrastructures. Because SMB is widely used and often provides access to critical business data, it is a frequent target for cyberattacks. Effective threat modeling helps organizations proactively assess risks and implement the necessary controls to defend against a wide range of attack vectors.

The first step in threat modeling an SMB network is to understand the assets involved and how they are accessed. SMB typically provides access to shared folders, files, and printers on a network. These resources may include sensitive data such as financial records, proprietary information, or customer databases. By identifying which SMB shares contain critical or sensitive data, organizations can prioritize these assets within the threat modeling process and focus their attention on the areas most likely to be targeted by attackers. Additionally, understanding who accesses these shares, whether internal employees, contractors, or remote users, allows organizations to map out the threat landscape based on user roles and privileges.

Next, it is essential to identify potential threats that could target SMB networks. One of the most common threats is unauthorized access by internal or external actors. Attackers often attempt to exploit misconfigured SMB shares that lack proper access controls or rely on weak authentication mechanisms. In such cases, unauthorized users could browse sensitive directories, exfiltrate confidential files, or plant malicious payloads in shared folders. Threat modeling must account for both deliberate actions by malicious insiders and external adversaries who gain network access through phishing, malware infections, or other means.

Another prevalent threat to SMB networks is the exploitation of vulnerabilities in SMB protocol versions or software implementations. Legacy versions of SMB, particularly SMB 1.0, are known to be vulnerable to remote code execution exploits such as EternalBlue, which was infamously used in the WannaCry and NotPetya ransomware attacks. These exploits allow attackers to compromise systems remotely, gain system-level privileges, and deploy malware across the network. Effective threat modeling includes evaluating which SMB protocol versions are in use, identifying unpatched systems, and considering how exposed these systems are to both internal and external attack surfaces.

Lateral movement is a key tactic used by attackers within SMB networks. Once an attacker compromises a single endpoint or user account, they often leverage SMB to pivot to additional systems within the network. This can be achieved through techniques such as pass-the-hash attacks, where stolen password hashes are used to authenticate to remote SMB shares without knowing the actual password. Threat modeling should examine potential lateral movement pathways, focusing on privileged accounts, open administrative shares like C$ or ADMIN$, and the level of segmentation between workstations, servers, and sensitive assets.

Denial-of-service (DoS) attacks against SMB services are another threat that organizations must consider. By overwhelming SMB servers with excessive traffic or specially crafted requests, attackers can degrade performance or cause service outages, disrupting business operations. In some cases, vulnerabilities may allow attackers to crash SMB services or the underlying operating system entirely. Modeling this threat involves assessing the resilience of SMB servers, their ability to handle high traffic volumes, and the existence of network-level protections to filter or mitigate malicious traffic.

Data integrity and tampering threats must also be included in the threat model. Attackers with write access to SMB shares may modify or corrupt files, introducing backdoors, ransomware, or other types of malware. They may also delete or encrypt important data to extort the organization or disrupt operations. Versioning, backup strategies, and file integrity monitoring should all be evaluated as countermeasures to these types of threats within the SMB environment.

Eavesdropping on unencrypted SMB traffic poses an additional risk, particularly in hybrid environments where SMB traffic traverses WAN links, VPN tunnels, or cloud networks. Attackers positioned within the same network segment as the client or server can intercept SMB packets to capture sensitive information, including usernames, passwords, or unencrypted files. Threat modeling must identify scenarios where SMB encryption or signing is not enforced and assess the risk of traffic interception, especially in networks with remote users or less secure network segments.

Man-in-the-middle (MITM) attacks are also a concern, where adversaries intercept and manipulate SMB communications between clients and servers. Without SMB signing or encryption enabled, attackers can alter SMB messages, redirect users to rogue file shares, or steal authentication credentials. The threat model should include an evaluation of how SMB sessions are protected during transit and how secure DNS and network segmentation can reduce the likelihood of successful MITM attacks.

The presence of third-party integrations or external-facing SMB services also introduces risks that should be accounted for. For instance, cloud-based file services using SMB, or SMB access exposed via VPNs to remote employees, may create new entry points for attackers. Evaluating the security posture of these external connections and how they integrate with internal SMB shares is a critical aspect of a comprehensive threat model.

Once threats have been identified, organizations must map them against existing security controls to identify gaps and prioritize mitigation efforts. Common controls include disabling outdated SMB versions, enforcing SMB encryption, restricting access to sensitive shares based on user roles, implementing SMB signing, and ensuring regular patch management. Threat modeling also emphasizes the need for logging and monitoring of SMB activity, using tools such as Security Information and Event Management (SIEM) systems to detect abnormal behaviors such as unauthorized file access, large-scale file deletions, or brute-force login attempts against SMB servers.

Threat modeling is an iterative process that evolves with the organization's infrastructure and threat landscape. As new technologies are adopted, such as hybrid cloud environments or virtual desktop infrastructures, the SMB threat model must be updated to reflect changes in exposure and business priorities. Additionally, incorporating threat intelligence from external sources, such as known attack patterns or indicators of compromise, enhances the relevance and accuracy of the model.

Ultimately, threat modeling for SMB networks empowers organizations to understand where their vulnerabilities lie, how attackers are likely to exploit them, and what proactive measures can be taken to reduce risk. It forms a foundational step in designing and maintaining a secure file-sharing infrastructure that supports business operations while withstanding the persistent threat of cyberattacks.

# Mitigating Man-in-the-Middle Attacks in SMB

Mitigating man-in-the-middle attacks in SMB environments is a critical aspect of maintaining the integrity and confidentiality of data transmitted across networks. SMB is a widely used protocol for file sharing, remote management, and printer access in Windows-based networks, but its extensive use also makes it a prime target for attackers. Man-in-the-middle, or MITM, attacks occur when a malicious actor intercepts communications between two legitimate parties, often altering or stealing data in transit without either party's knowledge. In SMB networks, this could involve attackers capturing sensitive files, authentication credentials, or injecting malicious payloads into file transfers. To defend against these threats, organizations must implement a multi-layered security strategy that addresses protocol-level vulnerabilities, network architecture, and authentication mechanisms.

The first and most fundamental step in mitigating MITM attacks against SMB traffic is to enforce SMB signing. SMB signing provides message integrity by adding a cryptographic signature to each SMB packet, ensuring that any attempt to alter the contents during transit is detected by the recipient. When SMB signing is enabled and required on both the client and server, any tampering with the SMB session, such as injecting malicious commands or modifying files in transit, will result in signature validation failures. As a result, signed sessions are terminated if an attacker attempts to interfere. Administrators can enforce SMB signing through Group Policy settings, requiring clients and servers within the domain to only accept signed SMB communications.

While SMB signing defends against tampering, it does not protect the confidentiality of data being transmitted. To address this, organizations should enable SMB encryption, introduced in SMB 3.0 and enhanced in later versions. SMB encryption encrypts the entire SMB session, ensuring that sensitive data, file contents, and even metadata such as file names and directory structures are protected from eavesdropping. Encrypted SMB traffic is unreadable to unauthorized observers, rendering intercepted packets useless to attackers. SMB encryption can be applied to specific shares or entire servers, allowing organizations to tailor encryption to protect critical data while optimizing performance.

Network segmentation is another essential defense against MITM attacks in SMB environments. By separating critical SMB servers and sensitive network segments from general user networks or guest networks, organizations limit the exposure of SMB traffic to potentially compromised devices. Using VLANs and firewall rules to restrict SMB traffic to specific subnets or trusted zones reduces the risk that an attacker can position themselves on the same network segment as their target. For remote users, connecting to SMB servers via a VPN or secure tunneling solution ensures that traffic is encrypted and protected as it traverses untrusted networks such as the public internet.

A critical factor in preventing MITM attacks is ensuring that name resolution services are secure. Attackers often use techniques such as NBNS or LLMNR poisoning to trick clients into resolving SMB server names to malicious IP addresses, redirecting traffic through rogue systems. To mitigate this risk, organizations should disable legacy name resolution protocols such as NetBIOS over TCP/IP and LLMNR on client devices and rely exclusively on secure DNS infrastructure. DNS Security Extensions (DNSSEC) can further enhance DNS integrity by ensuring that DNS responses are signed and validated. Implementing static DNS entries for critical SMB servers also reduces the likelihood of unauthorized name spoofing.

Credential security is equally important in mitigating MITM attacks. Weak or compromised authentication credentials are a primary enabler of successful interception and replay attacks. Enforcing strong password policies, utilizing complex and unique passwords, and implementing multifactor authentication (MFA) for administrative and privileged accounts can significantly reduce the likelihood of credential theft. Additionally, using Kerberos authentication wherever possible strengthens the security of SMB sessions, as Kerberos provides mutual authentication between clients and servers, reducing the opportunity for attackers to impersonate SMB servers or intercept authentication tokens.

Deploying network-based intrusion detection and prevention systems (IDPS) further protects SMB environments from MITM attacks. IDPS tools monitor network traffic for patterns consistent with MITM techniques, such as abnormal ARP traffic, rogue DHCP responses, or sudden increases in SMB session resets. By detecting suspicious behavior in real time, security teams can take corrective actions such as isolating compromised devices, blocking rogue traffic sources, and investigating the scope of the incident before damage is done.

TLS tunnels or IPsec VPNs can also be used to secure SMB traffic. By encapsulating SMB sessions within a secure tunnel, organizations can ensure that even if attackers are present on the same network segment, the encrypted tunnel prevents them from accessing the SMB payload. Site-to-site VPNs are commonly used to protect SMB traffic between branch offices and central data centers, while remote users typically access SMB shares through client-based VPN solutions. Some organizations are beginning to adopt SMB over QUIC, a modern transport that runs SMB within an encrypted QUIC tunnel over UDP 443, offering enhanced security and bypassing common firewall restrictions while reducing the reliance on traditional VPNs.

Administrative shares, such as C$, ADMIN$, and IPC$, can also present risks if left open and accessible to unnecessary users. MITM attackers who capture administrative credentials may target these hidden shares to move laterally, plant malware, or exfiltrate sensitive data. Limiting administrative share access to a tightly controlled group of trusted administrators and segmenting their access further reduces exposure.

Regular security assessments and penetration testing are vital for identifying weaknesses in SMB configurations that could be exploited in a MITM scenario. Ethical hackers and red teams can simulate real-world attacks, including traffic interception, rogue server deployment, and SMB relay attacks, providing organizations with insights into their defensive posture. Testing should include evaluating how well SMB signing and encryption policies are enforced and whether legacy or insecure protocols are still present within the network.

Lastly, user awareness and training are key components in preventing MITM attacks. Employees must be educated on the risks of connecting to untrusted networks, recognizing phishing attempts that lead to credential compromise, and reporting suspicious network activity. Combined with technical controls, a security-conscious culture minimizes the risk that users will inadvertently expose themselves to MITM threats.

Mitigating man-in-the-middle attacks in SMB networks requires a comprehensive and proactive approach. By implementing cryptographic protections such as SMB signing and encryption, strengthening authentication and credential management, and hardening the network against unauthorized access and spoofing techniques, organizations can significantly reduce the likelihood of successful MITM attacks. Consistent monitoring, testing, and user awareness complete the defense strategy, ensuring that SMB traffic remains secure and resilient in today's complex threat landscape.

# Zero Trust Approach for SMB Networks

The Zero Trust approach for SMB networks marks a significant shift in how organizations secure file sharing, resource access, and network communications. Traditionally, SMB networks have operated on a trust-based model, where users and devices within the internal network perimeter are considered trustworthy by default. This legacy approach, while effective in isolated or highly controlled environments, has proven insufficient in the face of modern cyber threats such as ransomware, insider threats, and lateral movement by adversaries who bypass traditional perimeter defenses. Zero Trust fundamentally rejects the notion of implicit trust based on network location, instead enforcing strict identity verification, granular access control, and continuous monitoring of every device, user, and transaction within the network.

Applying Zero Trust principles to SMB networks begins with eliminating implicit trust even within the internal network. In a Zero Trust architecture, access to SMB shares is tightly controlled based on clearly defined user roles, device posture, and contextual factors such as location or time of access. The first step is to integrate strong identity and access management (IAM) practices that leverage centralized authentication mechanisms, such as Active Directory combined with multifactor authentication, to verify user identities. Multifactor authentication prevents attackers from easily accessing SMB shares using stolen credentials alone, adding an extra barrier even when usernames and passwords have been compromised.

Once users are authenticated, Zero Trust dictates that access to SMB resources be granted on the principle of least privilege. This means that users and applications are only given the minimum permissions necessary to perform their tasks. SMB shares should be configured with fine-grained access controls using NTFS permissions or Access Control Lists (ACLs), ensuring that sensitive directories and files are only accessible to authorized personnel. Administrative shares such as C$ or ADMIN$ should be restricted to select administrative accounts and further protected through network segmentation and role-based access policies.

Device trust is another core pillar of Zero Trust for SMB networks. Before a device is permitted to connect to SMB shares, its security posture must be evaluated. Organizations can implement endpoint detection and response (EDR) solutions or network access control (NAC) tools that verify whether a device is compliant with security policies. Devices that lack updated antivirus software, exhibit signs of compromise, or fail other health checks should be denied access or placed in restricted network segments. This device-centric approach helps ensure that even authenticated users cannot access SMB shares from compromised or untrusted endpoints.

Segmentation is a crucial strategy in Zero Trust architecture. In a traditional flat network, SMB traffic may flow freely between all users and devices, making it easier for attackers to move laterally once inside. Zero Trust enforces strict segmentation by isolating critical SMB servers, file shares, and sensitive assets into protected network zones. Microsegmentation, achieved through technologies such as VLANs, software-defined networking (SDN), or firewall policies, ensures that users and devices only communicate with the specific SMB resources necessary for their role. This containment strategy limits the blast radius of potential breaches and reduces the likelihood of widespread ransomware infections or data exfiltration.

Continuous monitoring and behavioral analytics are essential components of Zero Trust applied to SMB networks. Rather than relying solely on initial authentication, Zero Trust requires constant verification of user and device behavior. Security Information and Event Management (SIEM) platforms and User and Entity Behavior Analytics (UEBA) tools are leveraged to detect anomalies in SMB access patterns. Unusual activity, such as mass file deletions, unauthorized access attempts to sensitive shares, or file transfers to unauthorized destinations, can trigger automated responses to block access, quarantine endpoints, or notify security teams for further investigation.

Encryption of SMB traffic is mandatory in a Zero Trust environment to protect against data interception and man-in-the-middle attacks. SMB 3.x supports end-to-end encryption, which must be enforced to secure data in transit across both internal and external networks. Encrypted SMB sessions ensure that sensitive information, such as intellectual property or personal data, is protected from eavesdropping or tampering, even when traversing less secure network segments or hybrid cloud environments.

Zero Trust also emphasizes the verification of network services and infrastructure. In an SMB network, DNS plays a critical role in resolving file server names to IP addresses. Attackers often exploit weaknesses in name resolution protocols, using techniques such as DNS spoofing or LLMNR poisoning to redirect SMB traffic to rogue systems. To prevent such attacks, organizations should disable legacy name resolution services like LLMNR and NetBIOS over TCP/IP, enforce secure DNS practices, and implement DNS Security Extensions (DNSSEC) to ensure the authenticity of DNS responses.

Another key aspect of the Zero Trust model is the adoption of adaptive access controls. These policies dynamically adjust access rights based on contextual information, such as geolocation, device type, user behavior, or the sensitivity of the requested resource. For example, access to highly confidential SMB shares might require stricter authentication or be restricted when users are connecting from outside the corporate network. Adaptive controls provide the flexibility to tailor security measures based on risk factors, strengthening protection without unnecessarily impacting user productivity.

In hybrid and cloud environments, the Zero Trust model extends to SMB shares hosted on cloud platforms such as Azure Files or Amazon FSx. These services must be integrated into the broader Zero Trust framework by enforcing identity-based access controls, encrypting SMB traffic, and monitoring usage through cloud-native logging and security analytics. Consistent application of Zero Trust principles across both on-premises and cloud-hosted SMB resources ensures unified protection regardless of where data is stored or accessed.

Automation is a powerful enabler of Zero Trust in SMB networks. Security orchestration, automation, and response (SOAR) platforms can automate incident response actions based on predefined rules. For example, if anomalous behavior is detected on an SMB share, such as mass file encryption indicative of ransomware, automation workflows can immediately revoke access, isolate affected systems, and alert the incident response team. Automation reduces response times and limits the damage caused by fast-moving threats.

Implementing a Zero Trust approach for SMB networks is not a one-time project but an ongoing journey of continuous improvement. As threats evolve and network environments grow more complex, organizations must regularly reassess trust assumptions, review access permissions, update security controls, and refine detection capabilities. Combining Zero Trust principles with a security-aware culture that prioritizes user education and proactive risk management helps create a resilient SMB infrastructure capable of withstanding the increasingly sophisticated tactics of modern cyber adversaries.

# SMB Logging and Monitoring Techniques

SMB logging and monitoring techniques are essential for maintaining the security, performance, and compliance of enterprise file-sharing environments. As SMB is a core protocol used for accessing shared files, printers, and network resources, it is also a frequent target for attackers attempting to exploit vulnerabilities, steal data, or move laterally across a network. Comprehensive logging and proactive monitoring of SMB activity help organizations detect unauthorized access, identify misconfigurations, troubleshoot operational issues, and ensure that sensitive data is properly protected. Establishing effective logging and monitoring practices requires a combination of native SMB capabilities, operating system features, and external security tools.

The first step in building a robust SMB monitoring system is enabling detailed auditing at the file server level. On Windows servers, this process begins by configuring object access auditing through Group Policy or local security policies. By enabling audit policies for file and folder access, administrators can capture critical events such as successful and failed read, write, delete, and permission changes on SMB shares. These events are recorded in the Windows Security Event Log, where they can be analyzed to detect anomalies such as unauthorized access attempts, privilege escalation activities, or mass file deletions indicative of ransomware attacks.

Once auditing is enabled, administrators should apply auditing settings to specific files and directories on the SMB shares. Fine-grained auditing allows for selective monitoring of critical resources, reducing log noise while focusing on sensitive areas of the file system. For example, directories containing financial records, intellectual property, or personal identifiable information should have detailed access auditing applied, while less sensitive shares may only require minimal logging. Setting up granular audit policies enables organizations to balance the need for comprehensive monitoring with the overhead of managing large volumes of log data.

Another critical aspect of SMB logging involves tracking user logon and authentication activity related to SMB sessions. SMB relies on the Windows authentication system, primarily Kerberos or NTLM, to validate user identities when accessing file shares. Administrators can configure Windows to log events related to user logins, group memberships, and logon failures. These logs provide valuable insights into who is accessing SMB resources, from where, and under what circumstances. Repeated logon failures, particularly those originating from unusual IP addresses or involving privileged accounts, are common indicators of brute-force attacks or credential stuffing campaigns targeting SMB services.

Network-level monitoring is also a key component of SMB security. Using tools such as Windows Defender Firewall with Advanced

Security or third-party network monitoring solutions, administrators can log and analyze inbound and outbound SMB traffic on TCP port 445. By tracking which IP addresses are initiating SMB connections and which resources they are accessing, organizations can identify potential scanning activity, lateral movement, or unauthorized use of administrative shares. Integrating this data with Security Information and Event Management (SIEM) platforms allows for the correlation of network events with host-level logs, providing a holistic view of SMB activity across the environment.

SMB-specific telemetry can also be collected through PowerShell cmdlets such as Get-SmbSession, Get-SmbOpenFile, and Get-SmbConnection. These cmdlets provide real-time information about active SMB sessions, including connected users, client IP addresses, accessed shares, and open files. This data can be exported periodically or integrated into custom scripts that feed information into centralized monitoring dashboards. Administrators can use this visibility to spot unusual patterns, such as the sudden appearance of unfamiliar clients accessing sensitive shares or unusually long-lived SMB sessions that could indicate compromised systems.

Advanced monitoring solutions, such as Microsoft's Defender for Identity or third-party endpoint detection and response (EDR) platforms, enhance SMB monitoring capabilities by providing behavioral analytics. These tools can detect lateral movement techniques commonly associated with SMB abuse, such as pass-the-hash attacks, SMB relay attacks, or the exploitation of administrative shares for malware propagation. Behavioral monitoring leverages machine learning models and baselines to identify deviations from normal user and system behavior, generating alerts when suspicious activities are detected.

Storage system telemetry should also be part of an effective SMB logging strategy. Many enterprise storage solutions and NAS devices that expose SMB shares offer built-in logging features. These may include audit logs for file access events, system events related to storage performance, and authentication logs. Collecting logs from storage appliances helps organizations detect insider threats, failed access attempts, or abnormal data transfer patterns at the storage layer, complementing host-based and network-level monitoring efforts.

Cloud-based SMB services, such as Azure Files or Amazon FSx for Windows File Server, offer their own native logging capabilities. Azure Files integrates with Azure Monitor and Azure Storage Analytics to capture metrics such as read/write operations, transaction rates, and error counts. Amazon FSx provides integration with AWS CloudWatch and CloudTrail, enabling detailed logging of SMB file system activity, administrative actions, and access attempts. Organizations using cloud-hosted SMB services must ensure that these logs are collected, retained, and integrated into their centralized SIEM platforms to maintain consistent monitoring across hybrid environments.

To improve the effectiveness of SMB monitoring, administrators should define clear alerting and escalation policies based on detected events. For example, alerts can be configured for patterns such as access attempts from external IP addresses, sudden spikes in file modifications within sensitive shares, or repeated failures to authenticate to administrative shares. Automated alerting accelerates response times by notifying security teams in real-time, enabling them to investigate incidents promptly and reduce potential damage.

Log retention and compliance are also critical considerations. Many regulatory frameworks, such as GDPR, HIPAA, and PCI DSS, mandate the collection and retention of audit logs to support forensic investigations and demonstrate compliance. Organizations must define appropriate retention periods for SMB-related logs and ensure that logs are protected from tampering through secure storage, access controls, and regular integrity checks.

Finally, regular review and tuning of SMB logging and monitoring configurations are necessary to ensure that they remain effective as network environments and threat landscapes evolve. Security teams should conduct periodic log reviews to identify gaps in coverage, optimize audit settings, and refine detection rules based on lessons learned from past incidents and updated threat intelligence.

By combining host-level auditing, network monitoring, behavioral analytics, and cloud telemetry, organizations can create a comprehensive SMB logging and monitoring framework. This enables proactive threat detection, supports compliance initiatives, and empowers security teams to identify and respond to incidents before they escalate into major breaches or operational disruptions.

# Incident Response for SMB Breaches

Incident response for SMB breaches is a critical process that organizations must follow to contain, mitigate, and recover from security incidents involving the Server Message Block protocol. SMB breaches can be particularly damaging due to the sensitive nature of the data often shared across SMB file shares, including confidential documents, financial records, and proprietary business information. Threat actors frequently target SMB due to its widespread use, and successful exploitation can result in data exfiltration, ransomware deployment, or lateral movement across the network. A structured and efficient incident response strategy is essential to minimize the impact of an SMB breach and restore normal operations as quickly as possible.

The first phase of incident response is detection and identification. Early detection of suspicious SMB activity is vital in limiting the scope of an incident. Security teams must monitor logs, network traffic, and endpoint activity for indicators of compromise, such as unauthorized access to SMB shares, failed login attempts, unusual file transfer patterns, or the creation of unauthorized shares. Intrusion detection systems and SIEM platforms play a crucial role in correlating data from multiple sources to identify potential SMB-related security events. When suspicious activity is detected, analysts must assess whether it constitutes a breach or an anomaly that requires further investigation.

Once a breach has been confirmed, containment becomes the top priority. Containment strategies aim to limit the attacker's ability to move laterally or exfiltrate additional data. Depending on the severity of the incident, containment may involve isolating affected SMB servers from the network, disabling compromised user accounts, or blocking suspicious IP addresses at the firewall. If ransomware is detected encrypting files on SMB shares, immediate action is necessary to prevent further encryption of additional shares or systems. Isolating compromised hosts can help prevent the attacker from expanding their foothold within the network while preserving evidence for forensic analysis.

Following containment, the next step is to begin a detailed investigation to determine the root cause and scope of the breach. Analysts must review SMB logs, authentication records, and network traffic to establish how the attacker gained access, which shares or files were targeted, and whether data was exfiltrated. Identifying the entry point often involves tracing lateral movement patterns, such as the abuse of administrative shares like C$ or ADMIN$, the use of compromised credentials in pass-the-hash attacks, or exploitation of SMB vulnerabilities such as EternalBlue. The investigation should also include a review of how the attacker escalated privileges and which user accounts were involved in the breach.

Preserving evidence is an essential component of the investigation. Security teams must collect forensic artifacts, including event logs, SMB session records, memory dumps, and network packet captures. This information is crucial for understanding the attack chain, supporting potential legal action, and enhancing future defenses. Care must be taken to maintain the integrity of evidence by following proper chain-of-custody procedures and using specialized forensic tools to avoid altering the data.

Once the cause of the breach is fully understood, eradication efforts can begin. Eradication involves removing the attacker's access to the environment and eliminating any backdoors, malware, or persistence mechanisms left behind. This may require patching vulnerable SMB services, changing passwords for affected accounts, removing unauthorized users or shares, and rebuilding compromised servers. If the breach resulted from an unpatched SMB vulnerability, immediate deployment of security updates across the environment is critical to prevent further exploitation.

After eradication, the recovery phase focuses on restoring normal operations and validating that the environment is secure. Any affected SMB shares or servers should be carefully reviewed before being reconnected to the production network. Restoring data from clean backups may be necessary if files were encrypted or corrupted during the incident. Prior to fully resuming operations, security teams should conduct thorough validation checks to ensure that no residual malicious code or unauthorized access mechanisms remain within the network.

Communication is an important element of the incident response process. Internal stakeholders, including executive leadership, legal teams, IT administrators, and human resources, must be informed of the breach and the steps being taken to resolve it. In cases where sensitive customer or employee data has been exposed, organizations may also be required to notify affected individuals and regulatory authorities, depending on data protection regulations such as GDPR or HIPAA. Transparency and timely communication help manage reputational risk and demonstrate the organization's commitment to security and compliance.

Once the breach has been resolved and systems have returned to normal, the final phase is conducting a post-incident review. This phase involves analyzing the incident response process, identifying lessons learned, and implementing corrective actions to strengthen defenses. The post-incident review should assess whether detection mechanisms were effective, if containment actions were timely, and how communication and coordination among response teams can be improved. The organization should also evaluate its existing SMB security posture, identifying gaps in configurations, monitoring, or patch management that contributed to the breach.

Security awareness training may also be included in the post-incident review. Many SMB breaches result from human factors, such as users falling victim to phishing campaigns that lead to credential compromise. Reinforcing best practices through regular training helps reduce the likelihood of future incidents. Technical improvements may include enforcing SMB encryption and signing, applying stricter network segmentation, disabling legacy SMB versions, and implementing zero trust principles to limit the lateral movement of threats.

Testing incident response plans through tabletop exercises and simulated breaches is another important outcome of the review process. By simulating SMB-specific attack scenarios, organizations can refine their response procedures, validate the effectiveness of containment and eradication strategies, and improve coordination among technical and non-technical stakeholders involved in the response.

Incident response for SMB breaches is a continuous improvement process that combines technical expertise, organizational coordination, and proactive planning. As cyber threats evolve, organizations must regularly revisit and enhance their incident response capabilities to ensure they are prepared to effectively respond to and recover from SMB-related security incidents. A mature incident response framework not only minimizes business disruption and data loss but also builds resilience against future attacks targeting critical SMB infrastructure.

# Penetration Testing SMB Services

Penetration testing SMB services is a vital component of evaluating and improving the security posture of an organization's file-sharing infrastructure. The Server Message Block protocol is widely deployed in enterprise environments to facilitate resource sharing, making it a frequent target for attackers seeking unauthorized access, sensitive data, or an initial foothold for lateral movement. Penetration testing SMB services involves simulating real-world attack scenarios to identify vulnerabilities, misconfigurations, and weaknesses that could be exploited by malicious actors. Conducting these tests systematically provides actionable insights into how secure the SMB environment truly is and where improvements are necessary.

The first phase of penetration testing SMB services is reconnaissance and information gathering. During this phase, testers seek to identify SMB services exposed within the internal network or, in poorly secured cases, on the internet. Scanning tools such as Nmap are commonly used to probe for open TCP port 445, which is the standard port for SMB traffic. When performing a comprehensive scan, testers look for SMB services running on file servers, workstations, network-attached storage devices, and even legacy systems that might still have SMBv1 enabled. The reconnaissance phase also focuses on collecting information such as SMB version, available shares, and server banners, which may reveal the underlying operating system version and patch level.

Following initial discovery, enumeration is the next step in penetration testing SMB services. Enumeration involves gathering detailed information about SMB shares, user accounts, groups, and file permissions. Tools such as enum4linux, rpcclient, and SMBclient are used to enumerate shares, retrieve user lists, and identify misconfigured access controls. Testers often look for shares with weak permissions, such as those accessible to Everyone or Authenticated Users, which could expose sensitive files to unauthorized users. During enumeration, testers also attempt to identify null sessions, where SMB services allow anonymous connections without requiring authentication. Null sessions can enable attackers to collect valuable information about the network's structure, such as domain users and shared resources, which could be used in later stages of the attack.

Once enumeration is complete, penetration testers proceed to authentication attacks. This phase focuses on identifying weak credentials, poorly secured accounts, or password reuse patterns that could be exploited to gain unauthorized access to SMB shares. Brute-force attacks using tools like Hydra or Medusa are commonly employed to test for accounts with weak or default passwords. Password spraying attacks, which attempt a limited set of common passwords across many accounts, are also used to avoid triggering account lockout mechanisms. In organizations where legacy protocols are enabled, penetration testers may also attempt NTLMv1 downgrade attacks or leverage tools like Responder to capture NTLM hashes via LLMNR or NBNS poisoning.

If testers successfully obtain credentials, either through direct password guessing or by harvesting NTLM hashes, they attempt to authenticate to SMB shares and escalate their privileges. Privilege escalation scenarios often involve identifying shares that grant write permissions to users who should only have read access or misconfigured administrative shares accessible to standard user accounts. In some cases, testers may plant malicious payloads within writable shares, hoping that the payload will be executed by unsuspecting users or automated processes with elevated privileges.

Another critical aspect of penetration testing SMB services is the exploitation of known vulnerabilities. One of the most infamous examples is the EternalBlue exploit, which targets unpatched SMBv1 services and can result in remote code execution. Testers will check for outdated SMB services susceptible to such exploits and use frameworks like Metasploit to attempt controlled exploitation. While modern environments typically have SMBv1 disabled, legacy systems or shadow IT infrastructure may still expose such vulnerabilities. Testing for other vulnerabilities, such as SMB signing not being enforced or weak SMB session security settings, is also critical to understanding the organization's risk exposure.

In addition to vulnerability exploitation, testers assess the ability of the environment to detect and respond to simulated attacks. They monitor whether intrusion detection systems, endpoint protection tools, or SIEM solutions generate alerts in response to brute-force attempts, unauthorized share access, or exploitation attempts. This step is critical for evaluating the effectiveness of an organization's security monitoring and incident response processes.

During the testing process, penetration testers often simulate lateral movement by attempting to pivot from one compromised system to others using SMB. This involves leveraging stolen credentials or open SMB sessions to access additional file shares, sensitive data, or administrative systems. Tools such as CrackMapExec or PowerShell-based scripts like Invoke-SMBClient can facilitate lateral movement by automating the discovery of accessible shares and performing authentication attempts across the network.

Post-exploitation activities are also part of penetration testing SMB services. If testers succeed in compromising a system via SMB, they may attempt to extract additional credentials, escalate privileges locally, or exfiltrate sensitive files. For example, dumping password hashes from a compromised server's memory using tools like Mimikatz can enable further attacks on other systems within the network. Simulating data exfiltration, such as downloading sensitive documents from SMB shares, helps organizations evaluate their ability to detect and block unauthorized data transfers.

Finally, the penetration testing engagement concludes with thorough documentation of findings, including details about each vulnerability or misconfiguration discovered, proof of exploitation, and recommended remediation steps. Testers provide prioritized recommendations, such as enforcing SMB signing and encryption, disabling SMBv1, hardening share permissions, implementing account lockout policies, and improving segmentation of critical SMB servers.

Penetration testing SMB services provides a realistic assessment of an organization's defenses against threats targeting one of its most critical protocols. By identifying weaknesses before adversaries can exploit them, organizations gain valuable insights that inform strategic security improvements, ensuring the resilience of their SMB environments against increasingly sophisticated attacks.

# SMB in IoT and Edge Computing

SMB in IoT and Edge Computing has become an increasingly important topic as organizations expand their networks beyond traditional data centers and into distributed environments. The rise of the Internet of Things has introduced a diverse ecosystem of connected devices such as sensors, cameras, industrial control systems, and smart appliances, all generating and consuming vast amounts of data at the network's edge. Simultaneously, edge computing architectures aim to process data locally, closer to where it is generated, to reduce latency, optimize bandwidth usage, and improve responsiveness. In this context, the Server Message Block protocol continues to play a vital role by providing a familiar and efficient mechanism for file sharing and resource access in distributed and constrained environments.

At its core, SMB enables devices to access and share files over a network using a common set of commands and conventions. In IoT ecosystems, edge gateways or micro data centers often serve as intermediaries between local devices and centralized cloud or enterprise systems. These gateways typically aggregate data collected from IoT devices and store it temporarily on local file systems before forwarding it to other locations for processing or archival. SMB provides a simple and effective way to share data between these edge nodes and IoT devices that support SMB clients, enabling local storage, file synchronization, and real-time data exchange in environments where direct access to cloud resources may not be practical due to connectivity limitations.

One of the reasons SMB is well-suited to edge computing environments is its compatibility with a wide range of operating systems, including lightweight Linux distributions and embedded Windows versions often found on edge gateways and IoT devices. Many of these devices operate in isolated or semi-connected environments, where direct cloud access is intermittent or unavailable. By leveraging SMB, edge devices can interact with local file shares hosted on gateways, performing read and write operations that facilitate data collection, firmware updates, configuration management, and log file transfers without needing constant internet access.

A common use case of SMB in IoT environments is in industrial automation, where Programmable Logic Controllers (PLCs) and Human Machine Interfaces (HMIs) rely on edge servers to store control data, operational logs, or production metrics. These edge servers often expose SMB shares to collect data from sensors or machine controllers. The data is then processed locally by the edge system and may be later transferred to a centralized data center or cloud platform for further analysis or long-term storage. This local data handling reduces latency and ensures operational continuity even in environments with unreliable WAN links.

In smart building environments, SMB is used to support file sharing between edge devices managing building automation systems, such as HVAC controllers, surveillance cameras, and energy management systems. Edge servers with SMB shares can centralize data such as access logs, video footage, or system configurations, enabling building management applications to process and respond to real-time events. For example, surveillance cameras may upload video files to an SMB share on an edge server for immediate access by security teams, without relying on a remote data center for storage and retrieval.

Security is a major consideration when deploying SMB in IoT and edge environments. Many edge devices are deployed in environments with less physical security, increasing the risk of tampering or unauthorized access. Furthermore, some legacy IoT devices may lack robust security features, making them vulnerable entry points for attackers. To mitigate these risks, organizations must enforce SMB encryption to protect data in transit between edge devices and gateways. Using SMB 3.x with encryption enabled ensures that files shared over SMB cannot be intercepted or tampered with during transfer.

Authentication and access control mechanisms are also critical. Edge computing environments often operate in segmented networks with local Active Directory or lightweight directory services managing user and device credentials. SMB shares must be configured with strict access controls, granting only authorized devices and users the ability to access sensitive files. This is especially important in environments where multiple IoT devices from different vendors coexist, each with varying levels of security maturity.

From an operational standpoint, SMB's ability to handle offline scenarios makes it highly advantageous in edge and IoT contexts. Edge nodes may temporarily lose connectivity to the cloud due to network disruptions, but SMB allows local IoT devices to continue interacting with edge file shares, ensuring that data capture and operational tasks proceed uninterrupted. Once connectivity is restored, the edge system can synchronize locally collected data with cloud storage or centralized systems, maintaining the integrity of the overall architecture.

Edge computing solutions often rely on containerization technologies like Docker or Kubernetes to deploy services at the network edge. SMB shares can be mounted within containerized applications running on edge nodes, providing persistent storage for applications that require access to shared data or configuration files. This allows edge workloads to interact with SMB shares in a secure and scalable manner, facilitating data exchange between containerized services and the wider IoT environment.

Performance optimization is another factor to consider when deploying SMB in edge environments. Edge networks may have limited bandwidth compared to data center infrastructures. SMB features such as SMB Multichannel, when supported, can improve data transfer speeds by utilizing multiple network paths or interfaces. Additionally, SMB compression introduced in SMB 3.1.1 can reduce the amount of data transmitted over constrained network links, optimizing file transfers between IoT devices and edge servers.

Monitoring and logging of SMB traffic at the edge is critical to maintaining visibility and detecting potential threats or operational anomalies. Edge gateways should be configured to log SMB access events, track failed authentication attempts, and monitor unusual file access patterns. These logs can be forwarded to centralized security monitoring platforms or cloud-based SIEM solutions to ensure that even remote edge sites are integrated into the organization's broader security framework.

As edge computing becomes more integral to modern IT architectures and IoT deployments continue to grow, the role of SMB as a lightweight, versatile, and well-understood protocol remains significant. By bridging the gap between resource-constrained devices and more powerful edge nodes, SMB enables distributed environments to operate efficiently, securely, and with resilience to network disruptions. Whether supporting smart factories, autonomous vehicles, or remote infrastructure monitoring, SMB in IoT and edge computing environments delivers familiar and reliable file-sharing capabilities that are essential for data-driven operations at the network's edge.

# Legal and Compliance Considerations with SMB

Legal and compliance considerations with SMB are becoming increasingly critical as organizations continue to rely on this protocol for file sharing and resource access across internal and external networks. The Server Message Block protocol, while essential for facilitating data exchange in enterprise environments, also presents legal and regulatory challenges due to its role in handling sensitive, regulated, and proprietary information. Ensuring compliance with local and international laws, industry regulations, and internal governance policies is essential for organizations to avoid legal penalties, protect stakeholder trust, and maintain the security and privacy of their data.

One of the most pressing compliance issues surrounding SMB is data protection and privacy. Regulations such as the General Data Protection Regulation (GDPR) in the European Union, the California Consumer Privacy Act (CCPA), and other regional privacy laws impose strict requirements on how organizations collect, store, and process personal data. SMB shares frequently host documents and files containing personally identifiable information (PII) such as employee records, customer data, financial details, and health-related information. Misconfigurations, such as publicly accessible shares or weak access controls, could lead to unauthorized disclosure of sensitive data and result in significant legal consequences. Organizations must ensure that SMB shares hosting regulated data are configured with strict access control measures based on the principle of least privilege and that sensitive information is adequately protected with encryption both at rest and in transit.

Compliance frameworks often mandate that organizations maintain detailed audit trails and logs for file access, modification, and deletion events on SMB shares. Regulations such as HIPAA, SOX, and PCI DSS require that organizations be able to demonstrate who accessed or altered sensitive data, when the activity occurred, and from where. Windows Server environments support file system auditing, which records access events within the Security Event Log, while third-party logging solutions can provide enhanced visibility into SMB activities. These audit logs must be securely stored and retained according to the applicable regulatory requirements, often ranging from several months to multiple years. Failure to implement effective logging practices may lead to compliance violations and hinder incident investigations.

Another key legal consideration involves data residency and cross-border data transfers. Many jurisdictions require that certain categories of data remain within specific geographic boundaries or comply with strict transfer mechanisms when data is moved across borders. For example, GDPR restricts the transfer of EU citizen data to countries without adequate data protection laws unless proper safeguards, such as standard contractual clauses, are in place. Organizations using SMB shares across multinational offices or cloud-connected environments must ensure that data replication, backup, or synchronization activities comply with applicable data localization requirements. Implementing controls such as geo-fencing, storage segmentation, or cloud-region restrictions can help organizations meet these obligations.

Retention and deletion policies are another area where SMB intersects with compliance. Various regulations require organizations to retain certain types of data for specified periods. For example, financial records may need to be preserved for several years under SOX, while GDPR requires personal data to be deleted when it is no longer necessary for its original purpose. Implementing automated data lifecycle management on SMB shares is necessary to ensure that data is retained and purged in accordance with legal requirements. Storage administrators should work closely with legal and compliance teams to define retention schedules and configure file expiration or archival mechanisms to enforce these policies.

Intellectual property protection is also a legal consideration for SMB environments. Many SMB shares store proprietary business information such as product designs, source code, research data, and trade secrets. Unauthorized access or data leakage of intellectual property can result in severe financial and reputational damage, and in some cases, legal disputes. Organizations must implement strong access controls, regular permission reviews, and encryption strategies to protect intellectual property on SMB shares. Legal teams may also advise on the necessity of confidentiality agreements, non-disclosure clauses, and contractual obligations with third parties who may have access to shared resources via SMB.

Third-party access to SMB shares introduces additional compliance risks. Vendors, contractors, and partners may require access to specific file shares to perform their duties, but extending SMB access to external entities increases the organization's attack surface and regulatory exposure. Organizations must perform due diligence on third-party security practices, ensure that data-sharing agreements comply with privacy regulations, and implement controls such as network segmentation, least-privilege access, and monitoring of third-party activities on SMB shares. Regulatory standards like ISO 27001 emphasize third-party risk management, and organizations should enforce these practices when granting SMB access to external users.

The use of legacy SMB versions, such as SMBv1, raises compliance concerns due to their known security weaknesses. Regulatory frameworks and industry best practices increasingly require organizations to maintain secure configurations and patch management processes to reduce cybersecurity risks. Running outdated or vulnerable versions of SMB may be considered a violation of regulatory requirements under standards such as NIST SP 800-53 or PCI DSS. To mitigate this risk, organizations must disable obsolete SMB versions, enforce the use of secure SMB protocols (such as SMB 3.x with encryption), and keep all SMB-related systems updated with the latest security patches.

Incident response requirements are another consideration. Compliance frameworks frequently require organizations to have documented procedures for detecting, responding to, and reporting data breaches or security incidents involving file-sharing systems such as SMB. Regulations like GDPR and HIPAA mandate notification to regulatory authorities and affected individuals within specific timeframes following a data breach. Organizations must ensure that their incident response plans include scenarios involving SMB breaches, such as unauthorized access, ransomware attacks targeting SMB shares, or data exfiltration via open file shares.

Employee training and awareness are also part of a comprehensive compliance strategy. Ensuring that users who access SMB shares are aware of acceptable use policies, data handling procedures, and the importance of securing sensitive files reduces the likelihood of accidental data breaches or policy violations. Regular training sessions and security awareness programs help reinforce compliance obligations and best practices when using SMB shares.

Finally, organizations must consider contractual obligations related to SMB-hosted data. Client agreements, service-level agreements (SLAs), and industry certifications may require that specific security and compliance measures are in place to protect data hosted on SMB file shares. These contractual requirements often include uptime guarantees, encryption mandates, data backup policies, and breach notification clauses. Legal teams must work alongside IT and security teams to ensure that the technical controls in SMB environments align with contractual obligations to mitigate the risk of legal disputes or reputational harm.

The intersection of SMB usage with legal and compliance obligations underscores the importance of designing, securing, and managing SMB environments with regulatory awareness in mind. Whether handling personal data, intellectual property, financial records, or sensitive business information, organizations must embed compliance considerations into their SMB architectures to ensure regulatory alignment, protect stakeholder interests, and support operational resilience in a dynamic and increasingly regulated digital landscape.

# SMB in Highly Regulated Industries

SMB in highly regulated industries plays a pivotal role in supporting the operational needs of organizations that must comply with strict legal, security, and privacy requirements. Industries such as healthcare, finance, government, and critical infrastructure depend on secure and efficient file-sharing mechanisms to manage sensitive information, ensure business continuity, and meet regulatory mandates. The Server Message Block protocol, widely used for file and resource sharing in enterprise networks, is deeply embedded in the IT ecosystems of these industries, facilitating access to confidential documents, patient records, financial statements, and other forms of regulated data. However, the use of SMB in such contexts requires a heightened focus on security configurations, access controls, and compliance-driven practices.

In the healthcare sector, the Health Insurance Portability and Accountability Act (HIPAA) mandates stringent requirements for the protection of electronic protected health information (ePHI). SMB shares in healthcare organizations often store medical records, lab results, billing information, and other patient-related data. To comply with HIPAA, healthcare providers must ensure that SMB file shares are secured through technical safeguards such as strong authentication, access control, and encryption. SMB 3.x supports encryption of data in transit, which is essential for preventing unauthorized interception of patient data as it moves across internal networks or between remote facilities. Additionally, healthcare institutions must implement robust auditing and monitoring mechanisms to track all access to ePHI stored on SMB shares, generating detailed logs that can be reviewed in the event of a security incident or compliance audit.

In the financial services industry, regulations such as the Gramm-Leach-Bliley Act (GLBA) and the Payment Card Industry Data Security Standard (PCI DSS) establish requirements for securing customer financial information and payment card data. SMB file shares in banks, credit unions, and insurance companies frequently house sensitive documents including loan applications, account statements, tax records, and underwriting data. To comply with regulatory mandates, financial institutions must enforce strict segmentation between public-facing systems and internal SMB file servers to minimize exposure to external threats. SMB shares should be restricted to authorized personnel based on their job roles, and sensitive data must be encrypted both in transit and at rest. Furthermore, multi-factor authentication should be enforced when accessing SMB shares that contain critical financial data to mitigate the risk of unauthorized access through compromised credentials.

Government agencies and contractors operating within the defense industrial base (DIB) or handling classified information must adhere to regulations such as the Federal Information Security Management Act (FISMA) and the Defense Federal Acquisition Regulation Supplement (DFARS). SMB shares used by these entities often store sensitive but unclassified (SBU) information, controlled unclassified information (CUI), or classified documents requiring special handling. Security guidelines outlined in frameworks such as NIST SP 800-171 and NIST SP 800-53 recommend the implementation of comprehensive access control mechanisms, strong encryption, and continuous monitoring of all file-sharing activities. SMB file servers in government environments must integrate with centralized identity and access management systems to ensure consistent enforcement of security policies, while security event logs generated by SMB servers must be reviewed regularly to detect unauthorized access or suspicious activity.

The energy sector, categorized as critical infrastructure, faces its own set of compliance challenges under frameworks such as the North American Electric Reliability Corporation Critical Infrastructure Protection (NERC CIP) standards. Power generation facilities, utilities, and energy providers rely on SMB to manage documents related to plant operations, maintenance schedules, engineering diagrams, and incident response plans. Given the potential impact of cyberattacks on the continuity of essential services, SMB file shares must be hardened against both external threats and insider misuse. This includes implementing SMB signing and encryption, segmenting operational technology (OT) networks from IT environments, and deploying intrusion detection systems to monitor for malicious SMB traffic.

Highly regulated industries must also address the threat of ransomware, which frequently targets SMB shares due to their centralized storage of valuable data. Ransomware actors often exploit misconfigured SMB permissions or leverage stolen credentials to encrypt files across entire organizations, disrupting critical operations and causing significant financial loss. To counter this threat, organizations in regulated industries must apply the principle of least privilege to all SMB shares, conduct regular permission reviews, and implement real-time monitoring tools capable of detecting and blocking ransomware behaviors such as mass file encryption or unauthorized file deletions.

Incident response capabilities are critical when using SMB in highly regulated industries. Many regulatory frameworks, including GDPR and HIPAA, require organizations to notify authorities and affected parties within strict timeframes following a data breach. Organizations must ensure that their incident response plans specifically address SMB-related breaches, including steps for containment, forensic analysis, remediation, and reporting. Having detailed audit logs from SMB servers, combined with well-practiced response procedures, supports compliance and reduces the time required to recover from security incidents.

In addition to meeting industry-specific regulations, organizations must also align with international standards such as ISO/IEC 27001, which outlines best practices for information security management. SMB environments within regulated industries should be governed by documented policies and procedures that define acceptable use, security controls, and ongoing risk assessments. Periodic internal and external audits should be conducted to validate that SMB file-sharing configurations comply with applicable regulations and internal governance standards.

SMB's role in supporting collaboration and operational efficiency is undeniable, but in regulated industries, it must be balanced with a comprehensive approach to security and compliance. This includes leveraging advanced SMB features such as SMB Multichannel for performance, while simultaneously ensuring that these capabilities do not introduce security gaps. Moreover, regulated industries should consider the adoption of Zero Trust principles to minimize implicit trust in their SMB environments, requiring continuous verification of user and device identities before granting access to sensitive file shares.

Training and awareness programs tailored to the unique risks and regulatory requirements of each industry are essential for ensuring that employees understand the proper handling of sensitive data stored on SMB shares. Human error, such as inadvertently sharing confidential files or misconfiguring permissions, remains a significant risk in highly regulated sectors. Ensuring that staff at all levels are aware of their compliance responsibilities and the potential consequences of non-compliance is an important complement to technical controls.

Ultimately, SMB in highly regulated industries must be deployed and managed with a focus on security, resilience, and regulatory alignment. By combining technical safeguards, rigorous policy enforcement, and a proactive compliance strategy, organizations can leverage SMB to meet their operational needs while protecting sensitive information and maintaining adherence to the complex regulatory frameworks that govern their industries.

# Emerging Trends in SMB Security

Emerging trends in SMB security are reshaping how organizations approach the protection of file-sharing environments in response to evolving cyber threats, regulatory requirements, and technological advancements. The Server Message Block protocol remains one of the most widely used methods for sharing files and resources within enterprise networks, but its ubiquity has made it a persistent target for threat actors seeking to exploit vulnerabilities and misconfigurations. As organizations modernize their infrastructures and adopt hybrid and cloud-based environments, the landscape of SMB security is undergoing significant transformation to address both legacy risks and new attack vectors.

One of the most prominent trends in SMB security is the accelerated adoption of Zero Trust principles. Traditionally, SMB operated under the assumption that users and devices within the internal network perimeter could be trusted by default. However, as threat actors continue to exploit internal weaknesses and insiders become a growing concern, organizations are shifting towards a Zero Trust model. This model mandates that no user or device is inherently trusted and that all access to SMB shares must be verified and continuously validated. Integrating SMB file shares into Zero Trust architectures requires strict identity-based access controls, multi-factor authentication, and real-time monitoring of user activity to ensure that access is only granted to verified and authorized entities.

The migration to cloud-based SMB services is another key development influencing SMB security. Solutions such as Azure Files and Amazon FSx for Windows File Server are becoming popular among enterprises seeking to reduce on-premises infrastructure and take advantage of cloud scalability. While cloud-based SMB services offer integrated security features such as encryption, access control, and automated patching, they also introduce new challenges related to securing hybrid environments. Organizations must now focus on ensuring consistent security policies across both cloud-hosted and on-premises SMB shares. This includes securing traffic with VPN tunnels, enforcing centralized authentication via Active Directory Federation Services (ADFS) or Azure AD, and monitoring cloud-based file shares using cloud-native security tools to detect unauthorized access or misconfigurations.

Encryption technologies are evolving to meet modern security demands in SMB environments. While SMB 3.x introduced encryption capabilities to protect data in transit, the adoption of SMB Direct with

Remote Direct Memory Access (RDMA) technology is gaining momentum. SMB Direct reduces latency and improves throughput while maintaining encrypted communication between servers and clients. This technology is particularly beneficial in data center-to-data center file transfers, storage replication, and high-performance computing environments. Furthermore, SMB compression, introduced with SMB 3.1.1, has emerged as a way to reduce the volume of data transmitted across networks, optimizing both security and performance in bandwidth-constrained scenarios.

Another emerging trend is the integration of SMB security with advanced threat detection and response platforms. Endpoint Detection and Response (EDR) and Extended Detection and Response (XDR) solutions are being increasingly deployed to monitor and analyze SMB-related activity in real time. These platforms leverage machine learning and behavioral analytics to detect lateral movement, unauthorized access, and ransomware indicators on SMB shares. Security teams can use EDR and XDR data to correlate anomalous SMB traffic with endpoint behaviors, improving their ability to quickly detect and respond to advanced persistent threats (APTs) that attempt to exploit SMB services as part of their attack chains.

The growing risk of ransomware has also influenced new SMB security strategies. Attackers frequently target SMB shares to deploy ransomware, encrypt files, and disrupt business operations. As a countermeasure, organizations are implementing ransomware-specific detection mechanisms that monitor SMB environments for signs of mass file encryption, unusual file renaming patterns, or abnormal spikes in file deletions. Automated response capabilities are being integrated into SMB environments, allowing systems to suspend user sessions, isolate affected file shares, or trigger incident response workflows at the first sign of ransomware activity. These proactive defenses are critical in reducing the impact of ransomware attacks and limiting the spread of infections across the network.

Microsegmentation and network isolation techniques are gaining traction as part of broader efforts to harden SMB environments. By segmenting file servers into distinct network zones and applying strict firewall rules, organizations can reduce the risk of lateral movement by threat actors. Microsegmentation at the VLAN or SDN level ensures that SMB traffic is confined to authorized network paths and prevents attackers from easily pivoting to other critical systems. Additionally, more organizations are adopting role-based access models, where SMB share access is tailored specifically to user roles, departments, or project teams, further reducing the potential attack surface.

Automation and orchestration are playing an increasingly important role in SMB security. Security Orchestration, Automation, and Response (SOAR) platforms are being leveraged to automate routine tasks such as user access reviews, security patch deployments, and incident response actions related to SMB security events. By automating these processes, organizations can ensure faster remediation of vulnerabilities and reduce the risk of human error. For example, when an SMB server logs multiple failed login attempts from a suspicious IP address, automated workflows can immediately block the IP address at the firewall and trigger an alert for further investigation.

The integration of identity and access management (IAM) with SMB security is also evolving. Organizations are moving beyond basic Active Directory group-based permissions and adopting advanced IAM solutions that support conditional access policies, dynamic user provisioning, and real-time risk assessments. These technologies allow administrators to enforce contextual access decisions for SMB shares, such as restricting access to sensitive file shares when users log in from unknown devices or high-risk geolocations.

As supply chain risks and third-party access concerns grow, SMB security strategies now frequently incorporate vendor risk management frameworks. Organizations are reviewing the security postures of vendors and partners who require access to shared SMB resources. Enhanced monitoring of third-party activity on SMB shares, combined with stricter contractual security obligations, ensures that external parties adhere to the same security standards as internal users.

Emerging regulatory requirements are also shaping SMB security. Data protection laws such as GDPR, CCPA, and industry-specific standards like HIPAA and PCI DSS continue to evolve, influencing how organizations configure and manage their SMB environments. There is a heightened focus on ensuring data residency compliance, implementing encryption at all stages of the data lifecycle, and maintaining detailed audit logs for forensic investigations and regulatory reporting.

Finally, security awareness and cultural shifts within organizations are increasingly recognized as vital components of SMB security. Training users on the importance of secure file-sharing practices, recognizing phishing campaigns, and reporting suspicious behavior helps strengthen the human layer of defense. As remote work and hybrid models persist, educating employees on securely accessing SMB shares over VPNs or cloud platforms remains essential to reducing the risk of insider threats and accidental data exposure.

Emerging trends in SMB security reflect a broader shift toward integrated, automated, and proactive defense strategies. By combining advancements in encryption, threat detection, cloud integration, and Zero Trust principles, organizations are positioning themselves to better defend against sophisticated attacks while meeting evolving regulatory expectations. The future of SMB security will continue to be shaped by innovation, collaboration between IT and security teams, and the growing complexity of enterprise IT environments.

# Case Study: SMB Exploit Analysis

In this case study of an SMB exploit analysis, we will examine a real-world scenario where an organization fell victim to a critical SMB vulnerability, leading to a major security breach. The incident occurred in a mid-sized financial services firm that heavily relied on SMB file shares for its internal operations, customer document management, and daily workflows across multiple departments. Despite having security protocols in place, a lapse in patch management and network segmentation created a window of opportunity for an attacker to exploit a well-known SMB vulnerability.

The breach began when an external threat actor scanned the organization's external network perimeter and identified an exposed Windows Server running SMBv1 services on TCP port 445. The server, intended for internal use only, was mistakenly configured with a public-facing IP address and lacked the necessary firewall protections to restrict access to trusted networks. Compounding the issue, the server had not been patched against the infamous EternalBlue exploit, which targeted the SMBv1 protocol and allowed remote code execution by sending specially crafted SMB packets.

The attacker used a common penetration testing framework to deploy the EternalBlue exploit against the vulnerable server. The exploit successfully triggered a buffer overflow condition within the SMBv1 service, allowing the attacker to execute arbitrary code with SYSTEM-level privileges. The initial payload consisted of a reverse shell, granting the attacker remote command-line access to the compromised server. From this foothold, the attacker was able to disable endpoint protection software, elevate privileges further by extracting cached credentials, and begin reconnaissance within the internal network.

Once inside, the attacker leveraged SMB shares across several departments to identify valuable targets. Open shares with overly permissive permissions allowed the attacker to access sensitive financial records, employee personal data, and proprietary customer information without triggering immediate detection. The lack of granular access controls and failure to implement SMB signing left the organization's file-sharing environment vulnerable to manipulation. The attacker created unauthorized user accounts and moved laterally to other servers within the network using pass-the-hash techniques, exploiting NTLM hashes captured from memory dumps on the initial compromised server.

Over the course of several days, the attacker methodically accessed SMB shares on the human resources and finance department servers, exfiltrating data to an external command and control server. The lack of network segmentation enabled unrestricted access between user workstations and critical servers, making lateral movement simple and undetected. The organization's SIEM solution was configured to monitor firewall and VPN logs but lacked integration with SMB audit logs or endpoint monitoring tools capable of detecting suspicious SMB traffic patterns.

Eventually, the attacker deployed ransomware to the SMB shares of the finance and HR departments. By encrypting shared folders containing critical payroll information, tax documents, and customer contracts, the attacker effectively paralyzed business operations. The ransomware note demanded payment in cryptocurrency in exchange for the decryption key. At this point, the organization's IT and security teams became aware of the breach due to reports of inaccessible files and encrypted directories.

Incident response efforts were quickly initiated, starting with isolating the affected servers from the network and initiating forensic analysis. Logs revealed that multiple unauthorized SMB sessions originated from a single compromised server, with unusual access patterns detected across multiple shares. However, the lack of comprehensive audit trails limited the ability to determine the full extent of data exfiltration. Forensics confirmed the use of EternalBlue, as memory artifacts from the payload were recovered, along with evidence of stolen credentials and pass-the-hash lateral movement techniques.

The post-incident review identified several critical failures that contributed to the success of the attack. The most significant was the presence of an unpatched SMBv1 service that had remained active despite widespread knowledge of its vulnerabilities. The organization had previously postponed scheduled patching due to operational constraints and lacked an automated vulnerability management system to enforce critical updates across all servers. Additionally, improper firewall configurations exposed internal services to the public internet, a fundamental network security lapse.

The absence of SMB encryption and signing further exacerbated the risk, as the attacker could intercept and manipulate SMB communications without detection. Additionally, shares were configured with permissions that violated the principle of least privilege, granting broad access to entire departments instead of implementing more restrictive, role-based access controls.

The recovery process involved restoring data from offline backups, which fortunately had not been affected by the ransomware due to being segregated from the SMB network. The IT team rebuilt the compromised servers, applied all pending security patches, and disabled SMBv1 across the environment. The organization also implemented SMB signing and encryption to secure future file-sharing communications and segmented the network to limit lateral movement capabilities.

As a result of this incident, the company adopted a more proactive approach to SMB security, including the deployment of endpoint detection and response tools, integrating SMB logs into their SIEM, and enforcing regular vulnerability scanning and remediation cycles. Additionally, the organization launched a security awareness training program to educate employees on the risks associated with misconfigurations, social engineering, and insecure file-sharing practices.

This case study illustrates how a single vulnerability within an SMB environment can serve as a gateway for attackers to compromise critical systems, steal sensitive information, and disrupt business operations. It underscores the importance of rigorous patch management, strict access control, and continuous monitoring of SMB traffic. The lessons learned from this incident helped the organization significantly enhance its cybersecurity posture and resilience against similar threats in the future, emphasizing the critical need for diligence in securing SMB infrastructures.

# Case Study: SMB Implementation in Enterprise Networks

In this case study of SMB implementation in enterprise networks, we will examine how a large multinational corporation successfully deployed the Server Message Block protocol to support file-sharing requirements across a distributed and complex IT infrastructure. The organization, a global leader in manufacturing and logistics, operates in over twenty countries and maintains a workforce of approximately fifteen thousand employees. The company's business operations heavily depend on the seamless exchange of documents, blueprints, project files, and transactional data between regional offices, manufacturing plants, distribution centers, and remote employees. Prior to the implementation of a standardized SMB infrastructure, the organization faced significant challenges related to fragmented file-sharing systems, inconsistent security controls, and inefficient workflows that hampered productivity and collaboration.

The organization's IT leadership identified the need for a scalable, secure, and highly available file-sharing solution capable of supporting both local offices and global operations. The decision was made to consolidate all regional file servers into a centralized, enterprise-grade SMB environment that could integrate with the company's Active Directory domain and align with global security policies. The primary goals of the implementation were to ensure reliable access to shared resources, enforce consistent permissions and security settings, reduce operational complexity, and improve data governance.

The project began with a comprehensive assessment of the company's existing file-sharing landscape. Regional offices were using a variety of legacy systems, including outdated Windows servers running unsupported versions of SMB, mixed with ad-hoc file-sharing applications and locally managed NAS devices. This decentralized approach resulted in inconsistent access control practices, redundant data storage, and a lack of visibility into who accessed or modified critical files. The company's IT team also discovered that some offices were still utilizing SMBv1, exposing them to well-documented vulnerabilities and regulatory non-compliance risks.

To address these issues, the IT team designed a centralized SMB implementation using modern Windows Server infrastructure deployed within two geographically dispersed data centers to provide redundancy and high availability. The design included the deployment of clustered file servers utilizing Storage Spaces Direct, a feature that combined locally attached storage across multiple nodes into a highly available and scalable storage pool. SMB 3.1.1 was selected as the standard protocol to take advantage of security features such as SMB encryption, SMB signing, and SMB Multichannel for optimized network performance.

The implementation phase began with the gradual migration of data from regional offices to the centralized data centers. To ensure minimal disruption to business operations, the migration was executed in stages, starting with smaller branch offices and progressing to larger manufacturing plants and administrative headquarters. Data migration tools were employed to transfer files from legacy systems to the new SMB environment while preserving NTFS permissions and folder structures. Simultaneously, the IT team conducted a thorough review of access control lists to enforce role-based access policies based on user departments, job roles, and project teams.

Once the SMB infrastructure was fully deployed, the company integrated it with its global Active Directory environment to enable centralized authentication and access management. By leveraging Active Directory group policies, the IT team standardized user access to SMB shares across all locations. This ensured that employees accessing file shares from different regions would experience consistent permissions and folder structures while administrators retained full control over who could access, modify, or share critical business data.

To support global operations and address latency concerns for remote offices located far from the primary data centers, the company implemented Distributed File System (DFS) Namespaces combined with DFS Replication. DFS Namespaces provided a unified directory structure across all offices, allowing users to access SMB shares using a single, logical path regardless of their physical location. DFS Replication synchronized critical files between the centralized data centers and strategically placed branch office servers, reducing access latency and ensuring business continuity in case of WAN link failures.

Security was a top priority during the implementation. The IT team enforced SMB encryption to secure data in transit between clients and servers, especially for remote offices connected over MPLS and VPN links. SMB signing was mandated across the entire network to prevent man-in-the-middle attacks and data tampering. Administrative shares such as C$ and ADMIN$ were restricted to IT personnel only, and detailed audit policies were applied to monitor access to sensitive shares. The company also deployed intrusion detection systems to monitor SMB traffic patterns for signs of unauthorized access attempts or lateral movement by potential attackers.

Another key component of the implementation was integrating the SMB environment with the organization's existing backup and disaster recovery systems. Regular snapshots of file shares were taken and stored both on-premises and in the cloud using the company's hybrid backup solution. This ensured rapid recovery capabilities in the event of accidental file deletions, ransomware attacks, or system failures. The IT team also created retention policies aligned with industry regulations to govern how long data was retained on SMB shares and when it was archived or purged.

User training was essential to the success of the SMB implementation. The company launched a global awareness campaign to educate employees on new file-sharing procedures, proper data handling practices, and the importance of adhering to security protocols. By providing comprehensive training sessions and clear documentation, the IT team minimized resistance to the new system and improved user adoption rates.

Post-implementation, the company observed significant improvements in operational efficiency and security posture. Employees benefited from faster and more reliable access to shared files, regardless of geographic location, and collaboration across departments improved due to the standardized SMB infrastructure. IT administrators reported reduced overhead in managing file servers, streamlined permission management through Active Directory integration, and enhanced visibility into file access patterns through centralized logging and monitoring.

Overall, the successful implementation of SMB in this enterprise network demonstrated the value of a centralized, secure, and scalable file-sharing solution. The project delivered improved data governance, enhanced security, and operational agility, supporting the company's mission to drive global business growth while protecting sensitive information. The lessons learned from this case study serve as a blueprint for other organizations seeking to modernize their SMB environments and meet the evolving demands of today's interconnected enterprise landscape.

# Building a Secure SMB Architecture

Building a secure SMB architecture requires a deliberate and systematic approach to ensure that file sharing and resource access via the Server Message Block protocol are resilient against internal and external threats. As a widely used protocol for network file sharing in both Windows and mixed-OS environments, SMB has evolved significantly over the years to include robust security features, but these features must be correctly implemented and complemented by sound architectural decisions. Without proper configuration and ongoing management, SMB can become a vector for data breaches, ransomware, and lateral movement within enterprise networks.

The foundation of a secure SMB architecture begins with selecting the appropriate version of the SMB protocol. Modern environments must enforce the use of SMB 3.0 or higher to benefit from advanced security features such as encryption of data in transit and improved message signing algorithms. Older versions of SMB, particularly SMBv1, are vulnerable to several well-known exploits and should be completely disabled across the network. Ensuring that all client devices and servers are configured to negotiate only secure versions of the protocol mitigates the risk of downgrade attacks and compatibility issues.

A critical element of secure SMB architecture is identity and access management. The principle of least privilege should guide the assignment of permissions to SMB shares, limiting access strictly to those users and groups who require it for business operations. NTFS permissions should be applied in combination with share permissions to create a layered access control model. For example, sensitive financial records might only be accessible to a restricted finance group with read-write permissions, while all other users have no access. Regular reviews of access permissions help to ensure that outdated or overly permissive configurations are identified and remediated.

To further strengthen access control, integration with Active Directory should be leveraged to centralize authentication and user management. By using group policies, administrators can enforce consistent access rules, password complexity requirements, and multi-factor authentication for users accessing SMB shares. When sensitive data is involved, multifactor authentication is a critical control that prevents attackers from gaining unauthorized access even if they obtain valid user credentials.

Encryption is another cornerstone of SMB security. SMB 3.x supports encryption of SMB sessions, ensuring that file transfers and other communications are protected against interception and eavesdropping, especially when data is traversing untrusted or public networks. Administrators should configure SMB shares to require encryption by default, particularly for shares accessed remotely or by external partners. In addition to encryption in transit, sensitive data stored on SMB shares should be encrypted at rest using technologies such as BitLocker or other file system-level encryption solutions.

A secure SMB architecture also requires thoughtful network design. Network segmentation should be used to isolate SMB servers from general user networks and from segments that handle less trusted devices such as guest Wi-Fi or IoT systems. By placing SMB servers in dedicated VLANs with strict firewall rules controlling access, organizations can limit exposure and reduce the risk of lateral movement by attackers who compromise endpoints elsewhere in the network. For particularly sensitive environments, microsegmentation using software-defined networking can be employed to further restrict SMB traffic to only the devices and applications that need it.

Auditing and monitoring are essential to maintaining situational awareness and detecting security incidents in a timely manner. SMB servers should be configured with comprehensive audit policies that log file access events, permission changes, and failed authentication attempts. These logs should be collected and correlated in a centralized Security Information and Event Management (SIEM) system, enabling security teams to identify anomalous activity such as brute-force login attempts or mass file deletions that may indicate ransomware activity. Alerting thresholds and automated responses should be configured to reduce detection and response times.

In addition to monitoring access events, organizations should implement baseline behavioral analytics to identify deviations from normal usage patterns. For example, a user who normally accesses project documents during business hours should trigger an alert if they suddenly attempt to download large volumes of sensitive files late at night from a new geographic location. Behavioral monitoring complements traditional logging and provides deeper insights into potential insider threats or compromised accounts.

Resilience and availability are also key components of a secure SMB architecture. Redundant SMB servers should be deployed in a failover cluster configuration to ensure that file-sharing services remain available during hardware or network failures. High-availability designs can incorporate features such as DFS Namespaces and DFS Replication to provide a consistent namespace and ensure that data is automatically synchronized between primary and secondary sites. Regular testing of failover procedures and disaster recovery plans is crucial to validate that the SMB environment can withstand disruptions without impacting business operations.

Endpoint security plays a critical role in protecting SMB environments. Workstations and servers accessing SMB shares must be hardened with security measures such as endpoint protection platforms (EPP), application whitelisting, and host-based firewalls. Enforcing security policies on endpoints reduces the risk of malware infections that could be leveraged to attack SMB shares. Additionally, organizations should educate users on secure file-sharing practices, including the risks of storing sensitive data on unsecured shares or sharing files via insecure channels.

Patch management is fundamental to securing an SMB environment. Both servers and clients must be kept up to date with the latest operating system patches and security updates, particularly those addressing vulnerabilities in SMB services. Automated patching tools and vulnerability management platforms can assist in maintaining a secure baseline across the environment. Delays in applying patches have been directly linked to high-profile breaches where attackers exploited known SMB vulnerabilities.

Finally, secure SMB architecture should include well-defined incident response procedures tailored to SMB-specific threats. This includes having playbooks for ransomware scenarios, unauthorized access events, and data exfiltration incidents involving SMB shares. Response teams must be prepared to isolate affected servers, revoke compromised credentials, and restore data from backups when necessary.

By carefully considering each of these elements, organizations can build an SMB architecture that is resilient, compliant, and aligned with security best practices. A secure SMB deployment not only protects sensitive data but also supports business continuity and instills confidence in stakeholders that shared resources are being properly safeguarded. As cyber threats continue to evolve, a proactive and layered approach to SMB security will remain essential for modern enterprises.

# User Training and Awareness for SMB Security

User training and awareness for SMB security is a critical yet often underestimated aspect of protecting an organization's file-sharing infrastructure. While much attention is typically given to technical controls such as encryption, firewalls, and access management, the human element remains a persistent and exploitable vulnerability. SMB file shares are widely used in corporate environments for sharing sensitive data, collaborating across teams, and supporting daily business operations. As such, employees, contractors, and other users who interact with SMB shares must be equipped with the knowledge and skills necessary to safeguard these resources from misuse, negligence, and cyber threats.

The foundation of an effective user training program for SMB security begins with educating employees about the role and significance of the SMB protocol within the organization. Many users access shared drives and folders on a routine basis without understanding the underlying mechanisms or the security implications of their actions. Training sessions should clarify how SMB facilitates file access across networked systems, the types of data commonly stored on SMB shares, and the potential consequences of mishandling such data. By raising awareness of how critical SMB is to business operations, employees are more likely to approach file-sharing tasks with a heightened sense of responsibility.

Central to this awareness is teaching users about data classification and the importance of handling sensitive information correctly. Employees should be able to distinguish between public, internal, confidential, and highly confidential data and understand the specific handling requirements for each category. For instance, employees should be trained to recognize that customer data, financial records, intellectual property, and personal employee information are highly sensitive and require stricter controls when stored on SMB shares. Users must also be informed about policies governing the use of SMB shares, such as which file shares they are authorized to access, the importance of adhering to access control lists, and the appropriate procedures for sharing or modifying files.

A major focus of user training should be secure authentication practices when accessing SMB resources. Users need to understand the importance of creating strong, unique passwords and the risks associated with password reuse across multiple systems. Multifactor authentication should be presented not merely as a compliance requirement but as a critical safeguard against credential theft and unauthorized access to SMB shares. Training should emphasize that credentials, particularly those with administrative privileges, should never be shared between users and must be kept confidential at all times.

Additionally, users should be taught how to recognize and avoid social engineering tactics that could compromise SMB security. Phishing emails remain a common method for attackers to harvest credentials or deliver malware designed to target SMB environments. Through realistic simulations and interactive exercises, employees can learn to identify suspicious emails, malicious attachments, and deceptive links. Reinforcing this knowledge helps users develop a security-first mindset and reduces the likelihood that they will fall victim to phishing campaigns or other manipulation techniques that could lead to unauthorized access to SMB shares.

The risks associated with accidental data exposure must also be addressed. Many breaches occur not due to deliberate malicious actions but because of mistakes, such as copying sensitive data to an unsecured public share, misconfiguring folder permissions, or inadvertently sending a file to the wrong recipient. Training should highlight best practices for managing permissions, verifying the intended recipients of shared files, and reviewing folder-level access rights before creating new shares. Users should be encouraged to seek guidance from IT administrators when in doubt about the appropriate handling of specific types of data or the correct security settings for an SMB share.

Another critical component of SMB security awareness is educating employees on the importance of physical security. Unauthorized physical access to an organization's facilities or network-connected devices can lead to the compromise of SMB file servers or the unauthorized removal of data stored on shares. Employees should be trained to lock their workstations when unattended, report suspicious physical activity in office environments, and ensure that portable storage devices are used and secured in accordance with organizational policies.

In environments where remote work or bring-your-own-device (BYOD) policies are in place, user training should cover secure practices for accessing SMB shares over VPNs or other secure channels. Employees must understand the risks of using unsecured public Wi-Fi networks and be instructed to always use encrypted connections when remotely accessing file shares. Training should also include practical demonstrations of how to map network drives securely, how to properly disconnect from SMB sessions, and the importance of applying regular updates to their personal or company-issued devices to protect against vulnerabilities.

To reinforce accountability, organizations should integrate SMB security awareness into broader cybersecurity policies and employee handbooks. Regular refresher courses, workshops, and mandatory e-learning modules ensure that employees remain informed about the latest security threats, new organizational policies, and emerging best practices related to SMB usage. Training initiatives should be supplemented with practical assessments, quizzes, or scenario-based challenges to measure understanding and retention of the key concepts.

Management and leadership play a key role in fostering a culture of security awareness. When executives and department heads actively participate in and promote security training initiatives, they send a clear message that cybersecurity is a priority across all levels of the organization. Recognition programs that reward employees who demonstrate proactive security behavior or identify potential security risks can further encourage a positive security culture.

An often-overlooked but vital aspect of training is preparing users to respond appropriately during a security incident involving SMB shares. Employees should be trained to recognize signs of potential compromise, such as unexpected file encryption, inaccessible shares, or unusual system messages. They should know the correct steps to report such incidents immediately to IT or security teams and understand that swift action can mitigate further damage or data loss.

Finally, organizations should continuously evaluate the effectiveness of their SMB security awareness programs. Regularly collecting feedback from employees, conducting simulated phishing campaigns, and analyzing incident reports can help identify gaps in training and inform improvements to the curriculum. By aligning user education efforts with the evolving threat landscape, organizations can ensure that their workforce remains well-prepared to protect SMB file-sharing environments from both accidental errors and deliberate attacks. A well-informed and vigilant user base is a powerful defense mechanism that complements technical controls and strengthens the overall security of SMB infrastructures.

# Automation in SMB Security Management

Automation in SMB security management is becoming increasingly indispensable as organizations seek to enhance the efficiency, consistency, and reliability of securing their file-sharing environments. The complexity and scale of modern enterprise networks, coupled with evolving cyber threats, make it difficult to rely solely on manual processes to safeguard Server Message Block infrastructures. By automating repetitive and critical security tasks, organizations reduce human error, accelerate response times, and ensure that security controls are uniformly enforced across distributed systems and user populations.

One of the key areas where automation improves SMB security management is in user access control. Granting, modifying, and revoking access to SMB shares is a routine yet sensitive task that, if performed manually, can result in inconsistent permissions, misconfigurations, and privilege creep. Automation tools integrated with identity and access management platforms can streamline this process by automatically provisioning access to SMB shares based on predefined rules tied to user roles, departments, or projects. When employees join, move within, or leave the organization, their access to specific file shares is adjusted automatically, reducing the risk of orphaned accounts or excessive permissions. Automated access reviews further ensure that permissions are regularly validated and aligned with business requirements.

Patch management is another critical component of SMB security that benefits significantly from automation. Vulnerabilities in SMB protocol implementations or the underlying operating systems have historically been exploited by attackers to gain unauthorized access or deploy ransomware. Automated patch management systems can identify unpatched servers and workstations, deploy critical security updates without manual intervention, and enforce policies to ensure that all systems remain compliant with corporate security baselines. By reducing the window of exposure for known vulnerabilities, automated patching plays a vital role in preventing SMB-targeted exploits such as EternalBlue or SMBGhost from compromising the environment.

SMB share creation and permission management can also be automated through infrastructure-as-code principles. Scripts and configuration management tools such as PowerShell, Ansible, or Puppet allow administrators to define standard templates for SMB shares, including access controls, encryption requirements, and audit settings. This approach not only accelerates the deployment of new shares but also ensures that security policies are consistently applied across all SMB environments. For example, administrators can automate the creation of project-specific shares with read-only access for certain groups and full-control permissions for designated project managers, eliminating the risk of deviations from established security guidelines.

Automation extends to monitoring and alerting in SMB environments. Security Information and Event Management platforms can be configured to automatically collect and analyze SMB-related logs, including file access events, failed login attempts, and permission changes. By using automated correlation rules and behavioral analytics, SIEM systems can identify potential threats in real time, such as insider threats, brute-force attacks, or ransomware activity on SMB shares. When suspicious activity is detected, automated workflows can trigger predefined response actions, such as isolating affected servers, disabling compromised user accounts, or escalating alerts to security operations teams for further investigation.

Data loss prevention (DLP) strategies are also enhanced through automation. DLP tools can automatically scan files stored on SMB shares for sensitive data such as credit card numbers, personally identifiable information, or intellectual property. If policy violations are detected, the system can automatically block the file transfer, quarantine the file, or notify the data owner and security personnel. Automating DLP enforcement ensures that sensitive data does not leave the organization through unauthorized or inadvertent means, helping to maintain compliance with regulatory requirements such as GDPR, HIPAA, or PCI DSS.

In environments where ransomware is a persistent threat, automation provides critical defenses through behavioral-based detection and response mechanisms. Endpoint detection and response tools, integrated with SMB monitoring systems, can automatically detect anomalous behaviors such as mass file encryption, unusual file renaming patterns, or spikes in file deletions within SMB shares. Upon detection, automated playbooks can be executed to contain the threat by disconnecting affected users, rolling back files to their pre-encryption state using snapshots or backups, and initiating a full incident response process to identify and neutralize the source of the attack.

Backup and disaster recovery workflows for SMB environments also benefit from automation. Automated backup solutions can be configured to create periodic snapshots of SMB shares, replicate data to offsite or cloud locations, and test restoration procedures regularly without manual oversight. This ensures that data stored on SMB shares is continuously protected and that recovery point objectives (RPOs) and recovery time objectives (RTOs) are met in the event of data loss or system failure. By automating backup validation and reporting, organizations gain assurance that their SMB data protection strategies are functioning as intended.

Compliance reporting, often a labor-intensive process, can also be automated through the integration of SMB auditing systems with compliance management tools. Organizations can generate scheduled reports detailing access logs, permission changes, encryption usage, and other SMB security metrics required to demonstrate adherence to regulatory standards. Automating this process not only reduces administrative overhead but also minimizes the risk of non-compliance due to missing or incomplete records.

Security orchestration, automation, and response (SOAR) platforms further enhance automation in SMB security management by integrating multiple security tools and processes into cohesive workflows. SOAR playbooks can automate the end-to-end incident response process for SMB-related threats, from initial detection to containment, eradication, and recovery. For example, if a SOAR platform detects unauthorized access to a sensitive SMB share, it can automatically revoke user permissions, trigger forensic data collection, and notify stakeholders without requiring manual intervention.

Automation also plays a role in maintaining consistent encryption configurations across SMB shares. Scripts can be used to enforce SMB encryption policies, verify that encryption is enabled on critical shares, and remediate any deviations automatically. Automated checks ensure that data in transit remains protected and that security settings cannot be disabled or misconfigured by mistake.

Finally, automation supports the enforcement of secure file-sharing practices among users. Organizations can implement automated policy enforcement tools that prevent users from copying files to public shares, ensure that only authorized users can create new SMB shares, and prompt users with security warnings when they attempt to share sensitive data outside of approved channels. These automated controls reduce reliance on user discretion and foster a security-first culture.

Automation in SMB security management is a force multiplier that enhances security effectiveness while reducing the burden on IT and security teams. By automating repetitive tasks, ensuring policy compliance, and accelerating incident response, organizations can protect their SMB environments against evolving threats and streamline operations. As cybersecurity threats become more sophisticated, the role of automation will only continue to grow, enabling organizations to stay ahead of attackers while optimizing the security of their file-sharing infrastructure.

# The Future of SMB Protocols

The future of SMB protocols is being shaped by evolving security needs, technological innovation, and the changing dynamics of enterprise IT environments. Originally designed to enable file sharing within local networks, the Server Message Block protocol has evolved far beyond its early implementations to meet the demands of modern distributed systems, cloud integration, and security-first architectures. As organizations increasingly rely on hybrid and remote work models, cloud-based services, and performance-driven applications, the expectations placed on SMB are higher than ever. The protocol's next phases will need to address a wide range of challenges while continuing to serve as a dependable foundation for networked file sharing.

One of the key trends influencing the evolution of SMB is the need for enhanced security by design. Cyberattacks targeting SMB, including ransomware campaigns and lateral movement tactics, have exposed the vulnerabilities of legacy versions and outdated configurations. SMB 3.x introduced encryption of data in transit and integrity protections through signing, but as threat actors become more sophisticated, the next generation of SMB will likely strengthen its cryptographic capabilities. Emerging versions are expected to adopt more advanced encryption algorithms and key management frameworks that can integrate seamlessly with enterprise Public Key Infrastructure (PKI) solutions. This will help ensure that data exchanged over SMB connections is protected against both passive eavesdropping and active tampering, even in high-risk environments.

Another significant shift is the growing emphasis on cloud-native SMB implementations. As enterprises continue to migrate workloads to cloud platforms such as Microsoft Azure and Amazon Web Services, SMB protocols are increasingly being delivered as managed services integrated directly into the cloud ecosystem. The success of services like Azure Files and Amazon FSx demonstrates the demand for scalable, secure, and highly available SMB services that operate natively in cloud infrastructures. Future iterations of SMB will likely include enhanced support for hybrid deployments, allowing seamless interactions between on-premises file servers and cloud-hosted SMB shares without sacrificing security, performance, or administrative control.

The evolution of SMB is also being driven by the rise of edge computing and the need for low-latency, high-performance file sharing outside of centralized data centers. Edge nodes deployed in smart factories, retail locations, and remote offices increasingly require fast, secure file sharing capabilities between devices and local applications. In response, future SMB versions are expected to incorporate optimizations tailored to edge environments, such as reducing protocol overhead, improving connection resilience in intermittent network conditions, and providing more granular control over caching and synchronization mechanisms. These enhancements will enable edge devices to leverage SMB for collaborative processing and data storage closer to the source of data generation.

A major technological advancement influencing the future of SMB is the adoption of new transport protocols, such as QUIC. Microsoft's initiative to enable SMB over QUIC introduces a modern approach to secure file sharing that operates over UDP 443 rather than traditional TCP 445. This innovation bypasses firewall restrictions commonly imposed on SMB traffic and leverages QUIC's inherent encryption and multiplexing capabilities to enhance security and performance. SMB over QUIC provides an attractive option for organizations seeking to improve secure remote access to file shares, particularly in scenarios where VPN usage is impractical or where existing perimeter security policies limit SMB connectivity. As this transport mechanism matures,

SMB over QUIC may become the default method for remote file-sharing scenarios.

Performance and scalability are central considerations for the next generation of SMB. The growing volume of data, combined with the demand for real-time collaboration and high-throughput workloads, requires SMB to continue improving its efficiency. Future versions of the protocol may build upon existing innovations such as SMB Multichannel, which allows multiple network connections to be utilized concurrently for a single session, and SMB Direct, which leverages RDMA-capable network adapters to deliver low-latency, high-bandwidth transfers. Further enhancements could include smarter load balancing algorithms, automatic failover mechanisms, and adaptive tuning of session parameters based on network conditions to maximize performance while minimizing resource consumption.

The integration of artificial intelligence and machine learning into IT operations is also expected to influence SMB protocols. Intelligent monitoring systems will increasingly interact with SMB to provide deeper insights into file access patterns, detect anomalies, and optimize resource allocation. Future SMB architectures may support telemetry and analytics hooks that feed real-time operational data into AI-driven systems, enabling dynamic policy adjustments and predictive maintenance of SMB infrastructures. These capabilities will help organizations detect security threats faster, reduce operational inefficiencies, and deliver more responsive user experiences.

Another key driver of change is the focus on simplifying SMB administration in large-scale environments. As file systems grow more complex, managing permissions, auditing access, and maintaining compliance become increasingly challenging. The future of SMB will likely involve greater integration with automation frameworks and infrastructure-as-code tools, allowing administrators to define SMB configurations, access policies, and security controls in declarative formats. This shift will reduce the administrative burden of managing SMB environments, improve consistency across deployments, and enable rapid provisioning of secure file shares in both on-premises and cloud settings.

Regulatory compliance will also play a significant role in shaping SMB's future capabilities. As data protection laws and industry-specific regulations evolve, SMB will need to provide native support for compliance features such as detailed access logging, built-in data classification, and enhanced retention policies. These features will help organizations meet audit requirements and maintain transparency over how sensitive data is accessed and handled across distributed SMB environments.

User expectations are changing as well. End users increasingly expect seamless and intuitive access to file shares across a wide array of devices, including mobile platforms and thin clients. Future SMB implementations may introduce improved support for cross-platform interoperability, ensuring that users experience consistent performance and security whether accessing SMB shares from Windows, Linux, macOS, or mobile operating systems. This will further enhance collaboration and accessibility in diverse enterprise ecosystems.

Lastly, the future of SMB will be marked by a heightened emphasis on resilience and disaster recovery. Given the critical role SMB plays in enterprise operations, future protocol versions will likely include enhanced features for automatic failover, geo-redundancy, and rapid recovery from file system corruption or data loss. By enabling more robust replication mechanisms and continuous availability options, SMB will continue to evolve as a key pillar of enterprise infrastructure that supports business continuity under adverse conditions.

The trajectory of SMB is guided by the need to balance innovation with backward compatibility, security with usability, and performance with resilience. As organizations face increasingly complex IT environments and sophisticated threats, SMB protocols will continue to adapt, providing advanced solutions for secure, high-performance, and flexible file sharing across both traditional and emerging infrastructures. The evolution of SMB will not only enhance the protocol's technical capabilities but also solidify its position as a critical enabler of collaboration and data exchange in the digital age.

# Conclusion: Evolving SMB and Network Security

The ongoing evolution of SMB and network security is a reflection of how modern enterprises continue to adapt to an increasingly connected and threat-filled landscape. As organizations expand their digital infrastructures, embracing hybrid clouds, edge computing, and global collaboration, the role of SMB remains central to providing reliable and efficient file-sharing capabilities across heterogeneous environments. From its earliest days as a simple protocol for LAN file sharing to its current iterations supporting enterprise-grade encryption, session multiplexing, and cloud integration, SMB has grown into a critical component of modern IT ecosystems. However, its evolution has not occurred in isolation; it has been shaped by broader trends in cybersecurity, data governance, and digital transformation.

The need to secure SMB protocols has never been more urgent. Threat actors have consistently targeted SMB infrastructures to exploit vulnerabilities, perform unauthorized data access, and deploy ransomware. High-profile incidents such as the WannaCry and NotPetya outbreaks underscored how weaknesses in SMB configurations and outdated protocol versions could have devastating consequences on a global scale. In response, organizations and technology vendors have had to harden SMB through security-by-design approaches, enforcing strong encryption standards, signing requirements, and authentication mechanisms that align with industry best practices. The shift from SMBv1 to SMB 3.x represented a major leap forward, incorporating essential protections that have since become the baseline for secure file-sharing operations.

Yet, while protocol-level improvements have played a vital role, the broader concept of network security has expanded to address the full spectrum of risks facing organizations. The move toward Zero Trust architectures represents a paradigm shift that assumes no inherent trust within the network perimeter. SMB security must now operate within frameworks where every connection, request, and user session is continuously verified, authenticated, and monitored. This holistic approach reduces the attack surface by limiting SMB access to authorized users and devices while enabling real-time threat detection and rapid incident response capabilities. By embedding SMB within Zero Trust frameworks, organizations are able to more effectively counteract insider threats, supply chain risks, and external adversaries seeking to exploit networked file shares.

Another key driver in the evolution of SMB and network security has been the rise of automation and orchestration. Managing large-scale SMB deployments manually is both impractical and risky. Automation streamlines the deployment, configuration, and enforcement of security policies across SMB environments, reducing the likelihood of misconfigurations and accelerating the remediation of vulnerabilities. From automated patch management to scripted permission management and security event correlation, automation ensures that best practices are applied consistently across geographically distributed environments. It also enables faster incident response workflows, allowing organizations to isolate compromised systems, revoke access rights, and recover critical data with minimal downtime.

Cloud adoption has further influenced how SMB is deployed and secured. Services such as Azure Files and Amazon FSx for Windows File Server demonstrate how SMB has been re-engineered to thrive in cloud-native architectures. These managed offerings provide scalable and resilient file-sharing services while embedding security features such as encryption, access control integration with cloud identity providers, and advanced auditing capabilities. As enterprises increasingly operate in hybrid and multi-cloud environments, the ability of SMB to function securely across these landscapes is essential. This hybrid evolution requires organizations to balance legacy on-premises deployments with modern cloud-integrated SMB services, while ensuring security and compliance requirements are met across all infrastructures.

The modern threat landscape has driven an increased emphasis on proactive detection and response. SMB environments are now monitored continuously using SIEM platforms, EDR and XDR solutions, and behavioral analytics tools that can identify and respond to anomalous SMB traffic, suspicious file access patterns, and privilege escalation attempts. The correlation of SMB audit logs with broader network telemetry provides a comprehensive view of activity within file-sharing environments, allowing for rapid detection of attacks such as ransomware, data exfiltration, or lateral movement using stolen credentials. This integrated approach to monitoring strengthens network security by providing context-aware insights and enabling security teams to quickly contain and investigate incidents.

Organizations have also become more aware of the regulatory and compliance implications associated with managing SMB shares. Regulations such as GDPR, HIPAA, PCI DSS, and SOX impose stringent requirements on how sensitive data is stored, accessed, and protected. SMB security has had to evolve to incorporate controls that support compliance mandates, including encryption of data in transit, detailed auditing, and retention of access logs. Enterprises are expected to demonstrate that their SMB environments follow principles of least privilege, maintain data integrity, and prevent unauthorized disclosures of regulated data. Security teams must now consider how SMB configurations and network security practices align with industry standards and legal obligations across all jurisdictions where the organization operates.

The evolution of SMB is also tied to the increased reliance on remote work and decentralized access to enterprise resources. The COVID-19 pandemic accelerated the need for secure remote access to file shares, leading to wider adoption of solutions such as SMB over VPN, SMB over QUIC, and cloud-hosted SMB services that can be accessed securely from anywhere. This shift has permanently altered how organizations think about perimeter defenses, prompting security teams to focus on endpoint hardening, secure remote authentication, and encryption of SMB traffic outside of traditional LAN environments.

Looking forward, SMB will continue to evolve in response to emerging technologies and business models. The growing importance of edge computing, IoT integration, and distributed processing will require SMB to operate efficiently and securely in increasingly complex network topologies. Meanwhile, innovations in AI-driven security automation, identity management, and quantum-safe encryption will further shape the development of SMB protocols and associated security practices. SMB's continued relevance depends on its ability to adapt to these changes while maintaining the performance and compatibility needed to support enterprise operations.

The path forward for organizations using SMB requires a commitment to continuous improvement. This involves staying current with the latest protocol versions, integrating SMB security into broader network security and compliance strategies, and fostering a security-first culture through user training and operational discipline. By viewing SMB not as a legacy technology but as a dynamic and adaptable platform, enterprises can better position themselves to meet the challenges of the modern digital landscape.

SMB and network security are now more interconnected than ever, with advancements in one area directly influencing best practices in the other. The collaborative efforts of security professionals, IT architects, and technology vendors are shaping a future where SMB continues to serve as a secure, efficient, and trusted solution for file sharing and resource access, enabling organizations to thrive securely in an era of rapid technological change and evolving cyber threats.

www.ingramcontent.com/pod-product-compliance
Lightning Source LLC
LaVergne TN
LVHW022316060326
832902LV00020B/3507